WRITER-FILES

General Editor: Simon Trussler

Associate Editor: Malcolm Page

D0223023

File on
SHAW

Compiled by Margery Morgan

Methuen Drama

A Methuen Drama Book
First published in 1989 as a paperback original
by Methuen Drama, Michelin House,
81 Fulham Road, London SW3 6RB,
and HEB Inc., 70 Court Street, Portsmouth,
New Hampshire 03801, USA
Reprinted 1990

Typeset in 9/10 Times by
L. Anderson Typesetting
Woodchurch, Kent TN26 3TB

Printed in Great Britain
by Cox & Wyman Ltd, Reading

ISBN 0-413-15280-4

British Library Cataloguing in Publication Data
is available from the British Library

Contents

The theatre is, by its nature, an ephemeral art: yet it is a daunting task to track down the newspaper reviews, or contemporary statements from the writer or his director, which are often all that remain to help us recreate some sense of what a particular production was like. This series is therefore intended to make readily available a selection of the comments that the critics made about the plays of leading modern dramatists at the time of their production — and to trace, too, the course of each writer's own views about his work and his world.

In addition to combining a uniquely convenient source of such elusive *documentation*, the 'Writer-Files' series also assembles the *information* necessary for readers to pursue further their interest in a particular writer or work. Variations in quantity between one writer's output and another's, differences in temperament which make some readier than others to talk about their work, and the variety of critical response, all mean that the presentation and balance of material shifts between one volume and another: but we have tried to arrive at a format for the series which will nevertheless enable users of one volume readily to find their way around any other.

Section 1, 'A Brief Chronology', provides a quick conspective overview of each playwright's life and career. *Section 2* deals with the plays themselves, arranged chronologically in the order of their composition: information on first performances, major revivals, and publication is followed by a brief synopsis (for quick reference set in slightly larger, italic type), then by a representative selection of the critical response, and of the dramatist's own comments on the play and its theme.

Section 3 offers concise guidance to each writer's work in non-dramatic forms, while *Section 4*, 'The Writer on His Work', brings together comments from the playwright himself on more general matters of construction, opinion, and artistic development. Finally, *Section 5* provides a bibliographical guide to other primary and secondary sources of further reading, among which full details will be found of works cited elsewhere under short titles, and of collected editions of the plays — but not of individual titles, particulars of which will be found with the other factual data in Section 2.

The 'Writer-Files' hope by striking this kind of balance between information and a wide range of opinion to offer 'companions' to the study of major playwrights in the modern repertoire — not in that dangerous pre-digested fashion which can too readily quench the desire to read the plays themselves, nor so prescriptively as to allow any single line of approach to predominate, but rather to encourage readers to form their own judgements of the plays in a wide-ranging context.

Bernard Shaw was a master of the unexpected. Given the 'set-text' status accorded to a limited number of his plays — whose 'revival', as Susan Todd suggests on page 115, all too often presumes a corpse-like condition in the originals — not the least valuable function of this volume is its reminder of the sheer range of his total dramatic output, and of its often experimental form. Even Shaw's earliest plays were regarded as impossible to stage — hence those long, novelistic stage directions, for works which at first could only be brought to life on the printed page. As an established writer for the live theatre, Shaw remained scrupulous in his concern for the appearance of his work in print — and, ironically, the first acquaintance many of us had with the writer was through those chunky, matt-brown *Complete Plays* given away in their tens of thousands as inducements to subscribe to the *Daily Herald*. The unlikely prospect of the output of any present-day dramatist being thought likely to produce new readers for a popular newspaper reminds us both of the pulling-power of Shaw's name in his heyday — and, of course, of the changed cultural status of the theatre and, for that matter, of the printed word.

Thus, Shaw began writing in a century when the theatre could itself lay claim to have been the most popular mass medium of entertainment: and something of the tug between that tradition and the actuality of the theatre's increasingly elitist role in society can be traced in his work, and recognized in the paradox of the socialist stump-orator tamed by the qualified adulation of the higher bourgeoisie. Mix in Shaw's distinctly equivocal feelings about human sexuality, and a quirky philosophy in which 'creative evolution' anticipated altogether less defensible interpretations of the life force, and it is perhaps all the more surprising that the combination of sheer rhetorical cleverness and a consummate sense of theatre should have enabled him to battle through periods of disfavour and neglect to his present (perhaps undesirable) classic dignity.

Simply, then, Shaw's plays have survived because they *work*, and at his best — one thinks unoriginally but irresistibly of *Heartbreak House* — he can peel away the thin veneer of national sensibilities and inhibitions so as to reveal both their deep emotional subtext and (another paradox) a profound sense of the closeness of the naturalistic and the surreal. Whether or not Shaw still has anything to teach us about politics or economics is matter for lively argument: but it is surely undeniable that he has a great deal to teach us about writing plays.

Simon Trussler

1856 26 July, born in Upper Synge Street, Dublin, the only son and third child of an unsuccessful grain merchant, connected with the minor gentry, who was sixteen years older than his wife. Disappointed in her marriage and disgusted by her husband's drinking, Mrs. Shaw found fulfilment in music and left her son largely to the attention of servants.

1866 Mrs. Shaw's singing teacher, George John Vandeleur Lee, well known in Dublin as a conductor and presenter of amateur concerts and operas, joined with the Shaw family in moving to No. 1 Hatch Street and taking a summer cottage in Dalkey by Killiney Bay.

1867 Started as a day boy at the Wesleyan Connexional School, Dublin.

1868 Taken from the Wesleyan School because of his unsatisfactory progress. Went to a 'very private' school near Dalkey in the summer, then for seven months — to his shame and horror — to the Central Model School, Marlborough Street, attended mainly by the children of working-class Roman Catholics.

1869 Attended the Dublin English Scientific and Commercial Day School and began a lifelong friendship with Edward McNulty, a bank clerk and minor novelist.

1871 On leaving school at fifteen, became a clerk in a land-agency office.

1873 His mother, with his younger sister, followed Lee to London, then sent for the elder sister, Lucy. Mrs. Shaw and Lee never again lived under the same roof.

1876 Feb., resigned post and joined his mother and Lucy in England, following the death of his other sister. Both women followed careers in music, Mrs. Shaw mainly as a teacher of singing (privately and at the North London Collegiate School), Lucy as a professional singer in light opera.

1876–77 'Ghosting' for Lee as music critic to a satirical magazine, *The Hornet*.

1878 Jan.–Feb., wrote 'A Practical System of Moral Education for Females' (published posthumously as *My Dear Dorothea*).

1879 Began seven months' employment with the Edison

Telephone Company, writing his first novel (*Immaturity*, first published in 1930) in his spare time.

1880   Joined a debating society, the Zetetical, where he met Sidney Webb. Second novel, *The Irrational Knot*, written.

1881   Contracted smallpox. Further ghost-writing for Lee on musical topics. In May, began writing *Love Among the Artists*. Met and fell in love with Alice Lockett in summer.

1882   Heard lecture by the American, Henry George, and proceeded to read his *Progress and Poverty*, following this with the first volume of Marx's *Kapital*, in French.

1883   Completed writing of *Cashel Byron's Profession*, followed by *An Unsocial Socialist*. Made the acquaintance of the established critic and champion of Ibsen, William Archer, in the British Museum. Launched on a period of oratory in the socialist cause.

1884   Joined the recently founded Fabian Society, together with Sidney Webb. Began writing for the Society with *A Manifesto*, published this year. In collaboration with Archer, started work on a play, abandoned after first act. Mar.–Dec., serialization of *An Unsocial Socialist* in *To-Day* led to first meeting with William Morris.

1886   First book-publication of *Cashel Byron's Profession* in England. Two pirated editions appeared in USA. Became music critic to the new *Dramatic Review* and art critic to *The World* (until 1889).

1887   Now settled, with his mother, at 29 Fitzroy Square. *An Unsocial Socialist* appeared in book form. Start of serialization of *Love Among the Artists* in *Our Corner*. 3 Nov. ('Bloody Sunday'), took part in Trafalgar Square protest put down by police: he dated his belief in political gradualism from this experience.

1888   Under pen-name, Corno di Bassetto, started reviewing music for *The Star* (until 1890). Edited and contributed to *Fabian Essays in Socialism*. Series of philandering love affairs, until 1898.

1890   Became music critic to *The World*, articles appearing under his own name for the first time.

1891   First edition of *The Quintessence of Ibsenism*, based on a lecture given to a Fabian arts group.

1892   *Widowers' Houses*, his first performed play, presented by the Independent Theatre Club.

1893   Worked on manuscript of Sidney and Beatrice Webb's *History of Trade Unionism*. Wrote *Mrs. Warren's Profession*.

1894 *Arms and the Man* at Avenue Theatre, London, in a season presented by Florence Farr, financed by Miss Annie Horniman (who was to subsidize the early years of the Irish National Theatre Company at the Abbey Theatre, Dublin). Actor-manager Richard Mansfield presented the play in New York.

1895 Somewhat reluctantly supported the Webbs in the foundation of the London School of Economics at 10 Adelphi Terrace, under the flat occupied by another Fabian, Charlotte Payne Townshend. 'The Sanity of Art' published in an American magazine.

1896 Richard Mansfield scored a success in New York with Shaw's *The Devil's Disciple*.

1897 Became a vestryman (borough councillor) of St. Pancras.

1898 Failure of efforts to get his plays publicly produced in England led to publication of two volumes of *Plays Pleasant and Unpleasant*. Marriage to Charlotte Payne Townshend, celibate from early days.

1899 Shaw's *You Never Can Tell* was first production of newly-founded Stage Society.

1900 *Candida* presented by Stage Society, with Granville Barker as Marchbanks.

1903 Defeated as candidate for St. Pancras in election for the London County Council.

1904 26 Apr.–10 May, six matinees of *Candida* presented by Granville Barker at the Court Theatre, Sloane Square. Thereupon, Barker, with J. E. Vedrenne as business manager, took over the theatre in a deliberate challenge to the commercial West End: attacking the long-run system, replacing the actor-manager and 'star' system by an acting ensemble with a director seeking to be true to the authors' intentions, and fostering a new English drama. In the next three years, the Vedrenne-Barker company presented eleven plays by Shaw.

1905 Command performance of *John Bull's Other Island* by Court Theatre company at 10 Downing Street, before King Edward VII.

1907 Vedrenne-Barker enterprise was ended by financial pressure. Put up half the money to buy a weekly, *The New Age*, to be edited by Holbrook Jackson and A. R. Orage.

1908 Granville Barker presented *Getting Married* at the Haymarket Theatre.

1909 Involved in presentation of evidence to the parliamentary committee on theatrical censorship.

1910 *Misalliance* produced in a season at the Duke of York's Theatre, mounted by Barker jointly with the American impresario Charles Frohman, but terminated after death of Edward VII.

1911 *Fanny's First Play* given long run (anonymously) under Barker-Lillah McCarthy management at Little Theatre. Left Executive of Fabian Society after 26 active years.

1912 *Pygmalion* written. Beginning of famous 'affair' with Mrs. Patrick Campbell (for whom the role of Eliza was written).

1913 19 Feb., death of mother. *Androcles and the Lion* at St. James's Theatre, the last time Shaw, Granville Barker, and Lillah McCarthy were associated in a London production. Three unsigned articles by Shaw included in first issue of *The New Statesman*. Premiere of *Pygmalion* in Vienna, then in Berlin.

1914 Commercial West End success of *Pygmalion*, starring Sir Herbert Berbohm Tree and Mrs. Patrick Campbell. Publication of 'Common Sense about the War' as 28-page supplement to *The New Statesman*, marking the beginning of Shaw's wartime unpopularity in England.

1917 In close consultation with Sir Horace Plunkett, chairman of Irish Convention set up by Lloyd George to resolve the Home Rule problem. *How to Settle the Irish Question* (first published as articles in *Daily Express*) advocated a federation of Ireland with England, Scotland, and Wales. Divorce of Harley Granville Barker and Lillah McCarthy foreshadowed Barker's retirement from the theatre and the ending of his professional and personal association with Shaw.

1919 *Peace Conference Hints* intended to influence the treaty negotiations at Versailles.

1920 *Heartbreak House* had its first production in America. Blanche Patch became his secretary, remaining in that position for the rest of his life. Death of his sister Lucy.

1922 *Back to Methuselah* first produced in America.

1923 First production of *Saint Joan* in America.

1924 His popularity in England restored by the production of *Saint Joan* at New Theatre. 20 Nov., Shaw's first radio broadcast, reading *O'Flaherty, V.C.*

1925 First public performance in England of his long-banned play, *Mrs. Warren's Profession*.

1926 Awarded Nobel Prize for Literature (for 1925).

1928   Publication of *The Intelligent Woman's Guide to Socialism*.

1929   First Malvern Festival, organized and financed by Barry Jackson, opened with *The Apple Cart*.

1931   Visit to Russia (in a small group including the first woman MP, Lady Astor, a close friend of his later years) and meeting with Stalin. First of series of long sea voyages with Charlotte, during which he wrote the next group of plays.

1932   Publication of the fable *The Adventures of the Black Girl in Her Search for God*. *Too True to be Good* produced first in Boston, Massachusetts, then at Malvern.

1935   Made Freeman of the City of London. *The Simpleton of the Unexpected Isles* at the Malvern Festival.

1936   First performance (in German) of *The Millionairess* in Vienna.

1938   Ill with anaemia. Wrote additional material for Gabriel Pascal's film of *Pygmalion*. World premiere of *Geneva* at Malvern Festival, followed by long run in London and serialization in a national newspaper (*The Daily Herald*).

1939   *Geneva*, in translation, playing in Warsaw when Hitler invaded Poland.

1940   Wrote new material for Pascal's film of *Major Barbara*, and spoke the prologue to be used in American distribution of the film. The Shaws stayed in their country house at Ayot St. Lawrence after the bombing of their London flat.

1943   Death of Charlotte Shaw. Completed *Everybody's Political What's What?* which became an instant best-seller.

1945   Filming of *Caesar and Cleopatra* by Pascal with Shaw's co-operation.

1946   Ninetieth birthday celebrations, including being made a Freeman of Dublin and the first honorary Freeman of the Borough of St. Pancras. New postscript to *Back to Methuselah* on creative evolution, written for World's Classics edition.

1948   Contributed to Jubilee Edition of *Fabian Essays in Socialism*. King George VI and Queen Elizabeth attended a performance of *In Good King Charles's Golden Days*, at People's Palace, Whitechapel.

1949   Visited by Pandit Nehru. Completed *A Rhyming Picture Guide to Ayot St. Lawrence*.

1950   Joined British Interplanetary Society. 2 Nov., died, leaving a will which publicized his long interest in simplifying English spelling by a bequest of his royalties for the establishment of a new, improved alphabet. This was legally challenged and (except in a token way) set aside in favour of the other, main beneficiaries: the National Gallery of Ireland, the British Museum, and the Royal Academy of Dramatic Art.

Compiler's Note

The first performances of Shaw's early plays were commonly readings given to secure copyright in the texts. When possible, he arranged for the first performances of his later plays to take place outside England, often in translation. In his lifetime, he was rarely a dramatist of the West End commercial theatre. Accordingly, although the present 'Writer-File' lists all London revivals, it is necessarily selective in recording the production history of Shaw's plays in the regions, in the repertoires of touring companies, and abroad: even the Irish record is incomplete. (It may, however, be noted that *all* Shaw's plays have now been presented at the still-flourishing Shaw Festival held annually at Niagara-on-the-Lake, Canada.) Amateur performances are mentioned only when they were premieres, and radio and television versions not at all, though the best-known films are recorded. Nearly all the extracts are from contemporary reviews of productions: the Bibliography lists sources for more considered and scholarly commentary.

Shaw liked to direct — or at least copiously advise on — the first productions of his own works, normally without acknowledgement in the programme credits. Thus, during the Vedrenne-Barker seasons at the Court, sole credit in the playbills was given to Granville Barker, in practice the co-director. Nor is Shaw's name to be found among the production credits for the premiere of *Saint Joan*.

For material prior to 1950, I have been greatly indebted to the *Theatrical Companion to Shaw*, compiled by Raymond Mander and Joe Mitchenson (London: Rockliff, 1954). My thanks are also due to the Society of Authors, both for access to material in their files and for permission to quote extensively from Shaw's own writings, as also from those of Granville Barker and James Joyce.

a: Major Plays

Widowers' Houses

'A Didactic Reality Play' in three acts.

Written: 1892 (on basis of abandoned collaboration with William Archer, 1885); extensively rewritten: 1898.

First (private) production (original version): Independent Theatre Club at Royalty Th., London, 9 and 13 Dec. 1892 (dir. Herman de Lange; with Florence Farr).

First American production (revised version): Herald Square Th., New York, 7 Mar. 1907 (dir. Lee Shubert).

First public production in England: Miss Horniman's Company at Midland Th., Manchester, 7 Oct. 1907 (dir. Ben Iden Payne; with Charles Charrington as Sartorius and Mona Limerick as Blanche).

Revived: Clarion Players (socialist amateurs), Blatchford Institute, Liverpool, Apr. 1909.

First public production in London: Miss Horniman's company from Gaiety Th., Manchester, at Coronet, Notting Hill Gate, 7 June 1909 (dir. B. Iden Payne, with Mona Limerick, and Lewis Casson as Trench).

Revived: Abbey Th., Dublin, 9 Oct. 1916; Everyman Th., Hampstead, 4 Sept. 1922 (dir. Milton Rosmer, who also played Cockane), and 26 July 1926 at same theatre; Stage Society at Malvern Festival Th., 19 Aug. 1930 (dir. H. K. Ayliff; des. Paul Shelving; with Barry K. Barnes as Trench and Cedric Hardwicke as Lickcheese), trans. to Prince of Wales Th., London, 22 Mar. 1931; Arts Theatre Club, 2 Feb. 1949 (dir. Esmé Percy); Unity Th., London, 19 May 1956 (Merseyside Unity Th. company, dir. Jerry Dawson); Theatre Royal, Stratford, 15 Mar. 1965 (dir. Ronald Eyre; with Jack May as Sartorius); English Stage Company at Royal Court Th., 14 Apr. 1970 (dir. Michael Blakemore; with Nicola Padgett as Blanche, Robin Ellis as Trench); Belgrade Th., Coventry, 1974; Actors' Company tour of South America, 1975, and at Wimbledon Th., 30 Mar. 1976 (dir. Philip Grant; des. Robin Archer; with Simon Cadell as Trench, Ciaran Madden as Blanche); Mercury Th., Colchester, Feb. 1980; Bristol Old Vic, Sept. 1981 (dir. John Dove; des. John McMurray; with Timothy West as Sartorius).

First published: original version, Henry and Co., 1893; rewritten version, in *Plays Pleasant and Unpleasant*, Vol. I, 1898.

During a tour of the Rhine, young Dr. Harry Trench and his older companion, Cockane, make the acquaintance of Mr. Sartorius and his daughter, Blanche. The nouveau-riche Sartorius approves the romance between Blanche and the well-connected Trench. Back in London and visiting his beloved, Harry learns of the disreputable source of Sartorius's money from the latter's dismissed rent-collector, Lickcheese. He asks Blanche to marry him without any financial help from her father. Sartorius talks him round, revealing that Harry's own income has the same ultimate origin. But Blanche, having vented her fury on her submissive maid, and still ignorant that her father is a slum landlord, breaks off the engagement. Act III reverses the situation: Blanche discovers the truth; a newly prosperous Lickcheese shows Sartorius how repairs to his slum properties will prove lucrative. Trench goes along with the plan, and Blanche avidly claims him as her own.

[The] first two acts of the Rheingold [*original title of the play*] ... present a series of consecutive dialogues. ... The bathing place is impossible; and I don't see how the long lost old woman is to be introduced without destroying the realism and freshness of the play: she would simply turn the thing into a plot, and ruin it. ... The peculiarity so far is that there is only one female character, and her social isolation is essential to the situation. ... You will perceive that my genius has brought the romantic notion which possessed you, into contact with real life.

Shaw, reporting to William Archer what he had done with the latter's scenario for a play, 4 Oct. 1887, *Collected Letters*, I, p. 175-6

Why did I write it? Not because I wanted to write a play particularly, but because I wanted to show up the slums and the cash nexus between them and the squares. ... It makes me laugh now when I read it. ... It is so Scribesquely constructed that you can see its ribs sticking out all over it.

Shaw, to William Archer, 19 Apr. 1919, *Collected Letters*, III, p. 600

It has very considerable literary qualities — the power of cogent argument, a terse and trenchant style, a really fine irony. But, for all that, it is a bad play. ... Mr. Shaw's people are not dramatic characters at all, they are embodied arguments.

A. B. Walkley, *The Speaker*, 17 Dec. 1892

I admire the horrible flesh and blood of your creatures.

Oscar Wilde, note congratulating Shaw on his play, 9 May 1893,
Letters of Oscar Wilde, ed. R. Hart-Davis, 1962

The Shaw revival in Britain began on 15 Mar. 1965 with Ronald Eyre's production of *Widowers' Houses*. ... Shaw's first play had never found a place in the standard repertory. ... It helped that Shaw's study of slum landlordism arrived in the wake of the Rachman case, but the work itself was quite enough to demolish a whole swathe of Shavian preconceptions and reveal an alarmingly human face under the grinning mask. ... The snarl of the underdog echoes under the dialogue, witness the parvenu sniping at Cockane, the gentleman parasite. ... Sex is supposed to be a Shavian blind spot. That would have been news to spectators recoiling from the sadistically erotic Blanche, a bourgeois cousin of Strindberg's Miss Julie.

Irving Wardle, 'The Plays', in *The Genius of Shaw*,
ed. Michael Holroyd, Hodder and Stoughton, 1979, p. 143-4

The Philanderer

'A Topical Comedy ... of the Early Eighteen-Nineties.'
Written: as four-act play, 1893; revised as three-act play, 1898.
Copyright reading: Bijou Th., Bayswater, 30 Mar. 1898.
First (private) production: New Stage Club at Cripplegate Institute, London, 20 Feb. 1905 (with Milton Rosmer as Charteris).
First public production: Royal Court Th., 5 Feb. 1907 (dir. Shaw and Granville Barker; with Ben Webster as Charteris).
First American production: Little Th., New York, 27 Dec. 1913 (prod. Winthrop Ames).
Revived: Everyman Th., Hampstead; 29 Jan. 1923 (dir. Milton Rosmer, who also played Charteris) and 26 Dec. 1924 (dir. Milton Rosmer; with Claude Rains as Charteris); Macdona Players at Palace Th., Chelsea, 4 Oct. 1926 (dir. Esmé Percy); Royal Court Th., 20 Jan. 1930 (dir. Esmé Percy, who also played Charteris); Arts Th. Club,

7 Apr. 1944 (dir. Henry Cass); Mermaid Th., 27 Jan. 1966
(dir. Don Taylor; with Derek Godfrey as Charteris); Roundabout
Stage I, New York, 29 Sep. 1976 (dir. Stephen Hollis); National
Theatre at Lyttelton, 7 Sep. 1978 (original version, dir. Christopher
Monahan; with Dinsdale Landen as Charteris, Penelope Wilton
as Julia).

First Published: in *Plays Pleasant and Unpleasant*, Vol. I, 1898.

The discarded and jealous Julia Craven breaks in upon the love-making of Leonard Charteris and the widow, Grace Tranfield. Charteris defends himself by accusing Julia of being a fraud as a 'new woman'. When the fathers of the two women arrive together, Cuthbertson's profession of dramatic critic allows Charteris to point out the conformity of the evening's events to a conventional dramatic plot. In the anti-conventional ambience of the Ibsen Club, the disastrous effect of polarizing the sexes into cold intellect versus emotion appears more clearly, as Charteris works relentlessly to free himself from the demoralized Julia. He succeeds in tricking her into accepting marriage with Dr. Paramore, a scientist of very defective humanity who may be seen as a savage caricature of Charteris's own coldness.

The Philanderer is a dangerous play with a clever but ignominious leading part. The leading woman, also ignominious, must be beautiful, passionate, and a perfect terror in the way of temper.

Shaw, to Richard Mansfield, 22 Feb. 1895, *Collected Letters,* I, p. 486

[T]he I[ndependent] T[heatre] ... refuses to produce *The Philanderer* (written specially for it) because it is vulgar and immoral and cynically disrespectful to ladies and gentlemen.

Shaw, to R. Golding Bright, 10 June 1896, *Collected Letters*, I, p. 632

It is the best of my plays; and when I work it up with a little extra horse play it will go like mad.

Shaw, to Granville Barker, 28 Dec. 1906, *Shaw-Barker Letters*, p. 73

Though the salt has evaporated for this generation which knows not

Clement Scott, from the speeches of Cuthbertson and his talk about 'manly men and womanly women' ... still there remains a genuine exhilarating spirit of comedy ... while beneath all the farce lies a formidable sincerity, immensely and lastingly refreshing. ... It 'dates' only superficially. ... We are tougher-minded than its early audiences, but this only means that the ugliness of the spectacle of seeing Julia flayed inhibits less our enjoyment of the comic aspects of her exposure ... and we are able to notice, what escaped her contemporaries, namely, the withering light which is turned on the philanderer himself.

Desmond MacCarthy, *New Statesman and Nation*, 3 Jan. 1925, reprinted in MacCarthy, *Shaw*, p. 81-2

Christopher Morahan's production successfully demonstrates that ... embryonic Shavian themes are thoroughly integrated in a brilliantly funny play. ...

The people are too pitiable or disagreeable to be played straight. Instead, the Lyttelton company adopt an illustrative style, catching the essentials of a character's behaviour without surrendering to an alien identity. ...

Shaw decreed that his work should be played without pauses, but ... in this show ... again and again prolonged silences allow ironies and contradictions to crystallize in the air between a speech and a response. One reward is the clarity it brings to Shaw's long-term character effects. ...

Irving Wardle, *The Times*, 8 Sept. 1978

... He's showing us people crashing painfully into each other in a kind of blind man's bluff.

John Peter, *Sunday Times*, 10 Sept. 1978

... One of the many merits of Christopher Morahan's revival is that it forces those of my persuasion to ask themselves if they haven't over-simplified [Shaw's] dramatic stance. ... Shaw was more self-knowing than humanoid geniuses usually are.

Benedict Nightingale, *New Statesman*, 15 Sept. 1978

Mrs. Warren's Profession

A play in four acts.

Written: 1893-94, but not licensed for public performance in Britain until 1924.

First (private) production: Stage Society at New Lyric Club, 5 and 6 Jan. 1902 (dir. Shaw; with Fanny Brough, Madge McIntosh, and Granville Barker).

First US production: Hyperion Th., New Haven, Conn., 27 Oct. 1905 (dir. Arnold Daly, who also played Frank).

First licensed public production in England: Macdona Players, Prince of Wales Th., Birmingham, 27 July 1925 (dir. Esmé Percy; with Florence Jackson and Valerie Richards), then in repertory, Regent Th., King's Cross, London, 28 Sept. 1925.

First West End production: Strand Th., 3 Mar. 1926 (dir. Esmé Percy; des. Francis Bull; with Edyth Goodall and Carleton Hobbs).

Revived: Little Th., 6 Feb. 1928 (dir. Esmé Percy; with Leah Bateman); Court Th., 30 Mar. 1931 (dir. Charles Macdona; with Miriam Lewes, Rosalinde Fuller, and Wilfrid Lawson as Crofts); Lyric Th., Hammersmith, on tour, May 1943 (dir. Heron Carvic; with Betty Balfour and Ann Casson); Torch Th., 2 Oct. 1945 (dir. Eric Crozier; des. Elizabeth Agombar; with Constance Fechter, Olga Edwardes); Bedford Th., Camden Town, 27 June 1949 (dir. Douglas Seal; with Paul Daneman as Frank); Arts Th., 25 Jan. 1950 (dir. Roy Rich; des. Michael Warre; with Brenda Bruce as Vivie); Royal Court Th., 24 July 1956 (dir. Terence O'Brien; with Ellen Pollock as Mrs. Warren); Gaiety Th., Dublin, 1961 (dir. Gerald Healy); Hampstead Th. Club, 22 Apr. 1965 (dir. Philip Guest; des. Michael Young); National Th. Company at Old Vic Th., 30 Dec. 1970 (dir. Ronald Eyre; des. Alan Tagg and David Walker; with Coral Browne, Sarah Badel and Ronald Pickup); Abbey Th., Dublin, 27 July 1977; Watermill Th., Newbury, 14 Aug. 1980 (dir. Michael Elwyn; with Dawn Addams as Mrs. Warren, Penelope Beaumont as Vivie); Nottingham Playhouse, 1980-81 (with Judy Campbell as Mrs. Warren); National Th. at the Lyttelton, 10 Oct. 1985 (dir. Anthony Page; des. Patrick Robertson and Rosemary Vercoe; with Joan Plowright as Mrs. Warren, Helen Turner as Vivie); Harrogate Th., 23 Feb. 1989 (dir. Andrew Manley).

First published: in *Plays Pleasant and Unpleasant,* Vol. I, 1898.

The highly-educated Vivie Warren goads her mother into revelations about her dubious past. She is filled with admiration for the freedom from hypocrisy and grasp of the economic truth of women's position in society that allowed her mother to escape from poverty into wealthy independence. Mrs. Warren's

*partner, Crofts, tries to blackmail Vivie into marrying him, and
throwing over the happy-go-lucky Frank Gardner, by pointing
out her own continuing dependence on the profits of sexual
exploitation. Vivie retreats from all emotional involvement into
accountancy and legal work.*

Miss Janet Achurch mentioned to me a novel by some French writer
[Maupassant's *Yvette*]. ... She told me the story, which was ultra-
romantic. I said, 'Oh, I will work out the real truth about that mother
some day'. In the following autumn I was the guest of a lady of a very
distinguished ability [Beatrice Webb] — one whose knowledge of
English social types is as remarkable as her command of industrial and
political questions. She suggested that I should put on the stage a real
modern lady of the governing class. ... I did so; and the result was Miss
Vivie Warren.

Shaw, letter to *The Daily Chronicle*,
30 Apr. 1898

It was an exceedingly uncomfortable afternoon, for there was a majority
of women to listen to that which could only be understood by a minority
of men. ... And, sure as I feel that most of the women and a good many
of the men ... did not at first know, and finally merely guessed, what
was the woman's trade, I cannot withhold the opinion that the represen-
tation was unnecessary and painful. ... If Mr. Shaw had fully understood
the nature of Mrs. Warren's profession he would have left the play
unwritten or have produced a tragedy of heartrending power. Now he
has merely philandered around a dangerous subject ... and produced a
play of a needlessly unpleasant understructure to no useful end.

J. T. Grein, *The Sunday Special*, 12 Jan. 1902

The play is morally rotten. ...
    It defends immorality.
    It glorifies debauchery.
    It besmirches the sacredness of a clergyman's calling. ... And worst
of all, it countenances the most revolting form of degeneracy, by
flippantly discussing the marriage of brother and sister, father and
daughter, and makes the one supposedly moral character of the play, a
young girl, declare that choice of shame instead of poverty is eminently
right.

New York Herald, 31 Oct. 1905

You are wrong, believe me, about the long speeches. The easiest thing to do in public is a monologue. ... Why does nobody ever fail as Hamlet? ... The real difficulty in that scene is not Mrs. Warren's talking, but Vivie's listening ...

Shaw, to Ellen Terry, 10 Aug. 1897, *Collected Letters*, I, p. 795

The first thing we did was to observe every stage direction absolutely literally. ... Because there's a geometry in his stage directions. ... It's part of the creation of the play as it goes on. ... Up to the last two weeks of the rehearsal period we leaned on Shaw's staging, put pressure on it and explored the stage geometry as well as the words. ... And then we could stage turning it round a bit. ...

Mrs. Warren is a highly emotional play, highly charged. The characters go headlong at each other but ... the inner process which in some other play might come out in one expletive in the text is elaborately verbalized live. But what you cannot do is to put the passion of the expletive into the whole speech. You have to find some cool way of serving it up. ...

The characters. ... They're economically tied together and the source of their food is the only thing really they have in common. ... Mrs. Warren and Vivie. ... Mother and daughter, maybe, but they have the air of orphans. That is what I believe the play is about. A desolation alongside which Pinter looks cosy.

Ronald Eyre, quoted in Ronald Hayman, *Playback*, Davis-Poynter, 1973, p. 114-15

The dismay of her daughter, ... her rejection of her mother and setting herself up as the new woman in accountancy offers, ... I suppose, a conflict between the life of the senses and the life of the mind: ... even in Shaw's hands the life of the senses wins hands down in terms of humanity. ... Mrs. Warren, as played by Coral Browne, became a superb volcano, ... elegant yet coarse-grained (downright Australian, in fact, from time to time), ... a restless powerhouse of capitalized sex. I don't know whether any young actress could have held the audience's sympathy against this elemental force, or whether it is possible to make the girl sympathetic at all.

J. W. Lambert, *Drama*, No. 100, Spring 1971, p. 17

Just as there are no heroes and villains in Shaw, neither are there any small parts. ... [Vivie] has no alternative but to uproot herself from this society altogether, but at the expense of becoming what Shaw, in a supreme insult, called a 'private person'. As Miss Turner plays it, her survival is an ugly sight.

Irving Wardle, *The Times*, 11 Oct. 1985

Anthony Page's icily brilliant production of this great late-Victorian morality play takes its strength from the perception, often missed by actors and directors, that none of its characters is particularly likeable. ...

[Vivie's] suicide gesture in Act III is not one of Shaw's melodramatic aberrations, for she's not revolted at the idea of incest but at the hot breath of sexual excess which has now come too near her and touched the only person she more or less cares for. Shaw may not have known as much about women as Ibsen or Chekhov, but what he knew he handled like a master.

John Peter, *Sunday Times*, 13 Oct. 1985

An uncompromising, progressive, political piece, full of passionate conviction. And, sadly, it has a lot to say which is as great an indictment of our society as it is testament to Shaw's powers as dramatist. It is so rare to see such a serious and strong play about women ... that I left feeling something like euphoria.

Time Out, 17 Oct. 1985

What makes the play so moving ... is its human sympathy. The daughter's rejection of her fallible, good-hearted mother is almost unbearably painful.

Charles Spencer, *The Stage*, 17 Oct. 1985

Shaw ... introduces each scene by reading his extremely detailed stage directions. The effect is one that Brecht, who admired Shaw, would have appreciated. Andrew Manley's production is set in a museum in which female dummies ... become art exhibits. ... So that when Shaw tells us we are seeing the garden of a country cottage, what we are actually seeing is stage hands rearranging the plush chairs and ropes. ... We are constantly reminded that we are watching situations being played out. And this is precisely how Shaw must have wanted his play to work.

Albert Hunt, *The Guardian*, 25 Feb. 1989

Arms and the Man

'An Anti-Romantic Comedy' in three acts.

Written: 1894.

First production: Avenue Th., London, 21 Apr. 1894, in Florence Farr's
season, financed by Miss Horniman (dir. Shaw; with Alma Murray as
Raina, Yorke Stephens as Bluntschli, Florence Farr as Louka).

First US production: Herald Square Th., New York, 17 Sep. 1894
(dir. Richard Mansfield, who played Bluntschli).

First foreign-language production: in German trans. by Siegfried
Trebitsch, Freie Volksbühne, Berlin, 1903.

Revived: Savoy Th., 30 Dec. 1907 (dir. Shaw and Granville Barker,
who played Saranoff; with Robert Loraine as Bluntschli, Lillah
McCarthy as Raina); Criterion Th., 18 May 1911 (dir. Arnold Daly,
who played Bluntschli; with Margaret Halstan as Raina); Abbey Th.,
Dublin, 25 Oct. 1916; Duke of York's Th., 11 Dec. 1919 (dir. Robert
Loraine, who played Bluntschli); Birmingham Repertory Th., 2 Feb.
1920 (dir. E. Stuart Vinden; des. Paul Shelving); Everyman Th.,
6 Mar. 1922 (dir. Norman Macdermott; with Milton Rosmer as
Bluntschli, Isabel Jeans as Raina); Everyman Th., 16 Sept. 1926
(dir. George Carr; with Frank Vosper as Saranoff, Robert Loraine as
Bluntschli, Isabel Jeans as Raina); Everyman Th., 16 Sept. 1926
(dir. Geroge Carr; with Frank Vosper as Saranoff, Robert Loraine as
Bluntschli, Jeanne de Casalis as Raina); Court Th., 23 Dec. 1926 (dir.
Esmé Percy, who played Bluntschli); Old Vic Th., 16 Feb. 1931
(dir. Harcourt Williams; with John Gielgud as Saranoff, Ralph
Richardson as Bluntschli, Marie Ney as Raina, Dorothy Green as
Louka); Embassy Th., 15 July 1935 (dir. John Fernald); Somerville
and Hoar Shaw Repertory Company in 14-week tour, commencing
May 1943 (dir. Heron Carvic, who played Bluntschli, with Ann
Casson as Raina); New Th., 5 Sept. 1944 (Old Vic Company,
dir. John Burrell; des. Doris Zinkiesen; with Laurence Olivier as
Saranoff; Ralph Richardson as Bluntschli, Margaret Leighton as
Raina, Sybil Thorndike as Catherine Petkoff, Nicholas Hannen as
Major Petkoff); Gaiety Th., Dublin, 1947 (with Cyril Cusack as
Bluntschli); Bedford Th., Camden Town, 6 June 1949 (dir. Douglas
Seale for Donald Wolfit); Arts Th. Club, 25 June 1953 (dir. Alec
Clunes, who played Bluntschli, with Diane Cilento as Louka); Lyric
Th., Hammersmith, 20 July 1953 (Belgian National Theatre
Company, dir. Raymond Gérome, in French); Pitlochry Festival Th.,
21 May 1955 (dir. Maxwell Jackson); Cyril Cusack's Co. from Gaiety
Th., Dublin, at Paris Festival, 1960: Mermaid Th., 20 Mar. 1962
(dir. Colin Ellis; with Joss Ackland as Bluntschli); Th. Royal, Bury

St. Edmunds, 15 Oct. 1968 (dir. John Gorrie; des. Hutchinson Scott; with Dinsdale Landen as Bluntschli); Chichester Festival Th., 8 July 1970 (dir. John Clements; with John Standing as Bluntschli and Sarah Badel as Raina); Greenwich Th., 13 Apr. 1978 (dir. Robert Chetwyn; des. Peter Rice; with Felicity Kendal as Raina, Lewis Fiander as Bluntschli); Haymarket Th., Leicester, trans. Lyric Th., 15 Oct. 1981 (dir. Jonathan Lynn; des. Alan Tagg; with Richard Briers and Peter Egan); Lyceum Th., Edinburgh, 31 Oct. 1984; Royal Exchange Th., Manchester, 22 Dec. 1988, and on tour, 1989 (dir. Caspar Wrede; des. Di Seymour; with Catherine Russell as Raina).

Film: British International Pictures, Elstree, 1933 (dir. Cecil Lewis), premiered at Malvern Festival, 4 Aug. 1932.

Pirated for plot and libretto of *The Chocolate Soldier*, operetta with music by Oscar Strauss, first performed in Berlin, 1909, then Lyric Th., London, 1910. Converted into a musical, in German, first performed in Vienna, Oct. 1972.

First published: in *Plays Pleasant and Unpleasant*, Vol. II, 1898.

Bluntschli, a mercenary soldier, hides in Raina's bedroom during a retreat. His down-to-earth realism challenges her romantic view of war and of the gallant Sergius, her betrothed. When the truce is made, Bluntschli calls to return the coat in which he made his escape. During various farcical goings-on, two betrothals are dissolved and replaced by truer partnerships: between Raina and Bluntschli, on the one hand, and the servant Louka and Sergius, on the other.

I have made a desperate attempt to begin a real romantic play for F[lorence] F[arr] in the style of Victor Hugo. The first act is nearly finished; and it is quite the funniest attempt in that style of composition ever made. I am told that I have unconsciously reproduced the bedroom scene from [Hugo's] *Marion de l'Orme*, which I never read.

        Shaw, to Janet Achurch, 2 Dec. 1893, *Collected Letters*, I, p. 409

It is an open secret ... that Mr. Shaw held counsel ... with a Bulgarian Admiral ... and that this gallant horse-marine gave him the hints as to the anti-saponaceous prejudices of the Bulgarians, their domestic architecture, their unfamiliarity with electric bells ... which he has so religiously, and in some cases amusingly, utilized. ... Why confound the issues in this way, my dear G.B.S.? ... Your Saranoff and Bluntschli and

Raina and Louka have their prototypes, or rather their antitypes, not in the Balkan principalities, but in that romantic valley which nestles between the cloud-capped summits of Hampstead and Sydenham. Why not confess as much by making your scene fantastic, and have done with it?

William Archer, *The World*, 25 Apr. 1894

But my play is not a historical play in your sense at all. It was written without the slightest reference to Bulgaria. In the original MS. the names of the places were blank, and the characters were called simply The Father, The Daughter, The Stranger, The Heroic Lover, and so on. The incident of the machine-gun bound me to a recent war; that was all.

Shaw, in response to a questionnaire,
To-Day, 28 Apr. 1894

To me the scenes between Sergius and Louka are so much more deeply felt than those between Bluntschli and Raina that I had myself rather play Sergius than Bluntschli; and rather have the strong woman of the cast as my Louka than my Raina.

Shaw, to Granville Barker, 17 Nov. 1907,
The Shaw-Barker Letters, p. 110

No doubt the audience thought your performance fine; but it was quite infamous. You were simply collecting laughs, asking for them, waiting for them, and not pretending to do anything else except once or twice, when you forgot yourself and acted instinctively. ... The audience was just longing to be allowed to believe in the play, and you wouldn't let it. ... The scenes with Raina in [the first] act were breezy beyond description. You worked that attitude with one foot on the dais to death; and the harder you worked it the breezier you became. There was nothing to apeal to the woman or the sympathy of the audience. ... The third act was not so bad. ... But it was desperately wanting in variety. You were visibly scoring the whole time; and the end of that inevitably is that the score loses its value.

Shaw, to Robert Loraine, 14 Dec. 1919,
Collected Letters, III, p. 646-7

The London stage is transformed out of knowledge, almost overnight. ... The lure of repertory was needed to bring back to the stage players who had made their name on the screen and wanted to work from time to time in both forms of art. ... Their debt to the State should be admitted frankly. ...

Ralph Richardson is a fine broad actor, hard to cast in the play of commerce because he is neither handsome lead nor character man. ... He seems to discover himself completely in ... Bluntschli. ... A rich, serious laughter, echoed in the voice, is the undertone of his playing.

The triviality of *Arms and the Man*, in this present revival, proves to be its charm. We laugh at the Balkans with a good conscience, and the shafts of wit aimed at heroism fall lightly at the feet of the returning warriors. [You] would never guess that the comedy was serious in its generation — a subject for prefaces and the like.

Ashley Dukes, *Theatre Arts*, Jan. 1945

John Burrell had directed *Arms and the Man*, and so Tony Guthrie didn't come to see us until the second night ... and came to say ... 'Don't you love Sergius?' I almost came to a halt staring up at him. 'Love that stooge?' ...

Tony Guthrie in all the shows we had worked in together had never said anything to me of a dazzling philosophical nature, but had stuck to technicalities. But this night, he said something which changed the course of my actor's thinking for the rest of my life. 'Well, of course, if you can't love him you'll never be any good in him, will you?' ...

It took me the inside of that week to get on to the idea; by the end of it I loved Sergius as I'd never loved anybody. I loved him for his faults, for his showing off, his absurdity, his bland doltishness ...

Laurence Olivier, *Confessions of an Actor*,
Weidenfeld and Nicolson, 1982, p. 109-10

How well the play has stood the test of time, despite the claim of so many critics that the targets of Shaw's satire are happily obsolete. ...

What I believe the play is really saying (pre-Pirandello) is that we all adopt some kind of protective social mask which occasionally slips to reveal the genuine face beneath ... the player's, ... a fresh and relevant statement on the constant clash between our public and our private selves. ...

Mr. Standing's comic timing is excellent and he conveys very well the character's brisk, matter-of-fact common-sense. It's not his fault that he's forced to operate in something of a void.

Michael Billington, *Plays and Players*, Sept. 1970, p. 32

The Man of Destiny

'A Fictitious Paragraph of History' in one act.
Written: 1895.
First productions: Grand Th., Croydon,1 July 1897 (dir. Murray Carson,
who played Napoleon); Comedy Th., for special Sunday matinee,
29 Mar. 1901 (dir. Granville Barker, who played Napoleon).
First foreign-language production: Schauspielhaus, Frankfurt,
21 Apr. 1903, revived Neues Th., Berlin, 10 Feb. 1904
(prod. Max Reinhardt).
First fully professional US production: Vaudeville Th., New York,
11 Feb. 1904 (dir. and acted by Arnold Daly).
First public West End production: Vedrenne-Barker company,
Court Th., 4 June 1907 (dir. Granville Barker; with Dion Boucicault
and Irene Vanbrugh).
Revived: Abbey Th., Dublin, 9 Mar. 1922; Everyman Th., Hampstead,
27 Aug. 1924 (dir. Norman Mcdermott; with Claude Rains and
Jeanne de Casalis); Mercury Th., 7 Oct. 1938 (dir. Ashley Dukes);
Shaw Repertory Company on tour, Sept. 1942 (dir. Ronald Giffen);
Arts Theatre Club, 1 Dec. 1942 (dir. Stanford Holme; with
Walter Hudd); Th. Royal, Newcastle, 9 Feb. 1951, trans. St. Martin's
Th., 3 Apr. 1951 (dir. Ellen Pollock; with Karl Stepanek and
Rosamund John); Arts Theatre Club, 27 June 1951 (dir. John Fernald;
with Maurice Denham and Brenda Bruce); Malvern Festival Th.,
29 Aug. 1966 (dir. Terence Lodge; with Dudley Jones and Pamela
Ann Davy); Mermaid Th, 14 Sept. 1966 (dir. Robert Kidd; des. John
Gunter and Sheelagh Killeen; with Sian Phillips and Ian McKellen);
Open Space, 18 Jan. 1973 (dir. Jeremy Young; with Diana Quick);
Open Air Th., Regents Park, 17 July 1978 (dir. Richard Digby Day;
with Maria Aitken).
First published: in *Plays Pleasant and Unpleasant*, Vol. II, 1898.

---

*Resting at an inn two days after a battle, the young Napoleon
puts under arrest a junior officer who has been deceived into
handing over his dispatches by a youth he met on the road. A
young woman who arrives at the inn is recognized as the
'youth', and the core of the play is the ensuing verbal duel
between Napoleon and the Lady, which results in her returning
the dispatches — and Napoleon reading a private letter which
has got among them.*

The ... Napoleon piece — has practically never been offered to anybody, because Ellen Terry took a fancy to it, and Irving proposed to produce it and play Napoleon.

> Shaw, to Golding Bright, 10 June 1896,
> *Collected Letters*, I, p. 630

I gave him [Irving] the power to behave like a confidence-trick man if he liked, which he has accordingly done. ... Even now he has returned the play without returning my agreement. ... I will have nothing to do with him now. ... I don't care, and never did care who plays Napoleon (it was written for Mansfield); but I should have liked you to play the Strange Lady ...

> Shaw, to Ellen Terry, 11 May 1897, *Collected Letters*, I, p. 761

It is not exactly a burlesque: it is more a harlequinade, in which Napoleon and a strange lady play harlequin and columbine, and a chuckle headed, asinine young sublieutenant ... and an innkeeper ... play clown and pantaloon. The dialogue is all pure Shaw — nothing Candidesque or human.

> Shaw, to Janet Achurch, 24 Aug. 1895, *Collected Letters*, I, p. 546-7

The Man of Destiny is an enchanting play. ... Shaw's Napoleon is a realist adept at striking romantic attitudes. ... Shaw, the realist, unashamedly enjoyed theatrical hokum. ... His Napoleon is much more endearing than the later, disillusioned, Caesar: but there was never a dictator like that.

Ian McKellen plays him fluently and well, but misses out on the daemonic, Corsican side of the character: that last great speech needs the glow of mystery as well as the wit. ... Sian Phillips, on the other hand, seems to me to capture all the aspects of the Strange Lady ... in a performance of great charm.

> Frank Marcus, *Plays and Players*, Nov. 1966, p. 15

Candida

'A Mystery' in three acts.
Written: 1894-95.
Copyright reading: Theatre Royal, South Shields, 30 Mar. 1895
  (dir. A. E. Drinkwater).

First production: Independent Th. Company, Her Majesty's Th.,
Aberdeen, 30 July 1897 (dir. Charles Charrington; with
Janet Achurch).

First US productions: Fine Arts Building, Chicago, by students,
4 Apr. 1899 ; Browning Society, South Broad St. Th., Philadelphia,
18 May 1903.

First London production: Stage Society, Strand Th., 1 July 1900
(dir. Charles Charrington, who also played Morell, with Janet
Achurch, and Granville Barker as Marchbanks).

First fully professional US production: Prince's Th., New York,
8 Dec. 1903 (dir. and acted by Arnold Daly).

First public production in London: Court Theatre, 26 Apr. 1904
(dir. Granville Barker, who also played Marchbanks, with
Kate Rorke).

Revived: Vedrenne-Barker company, Court Theatre, 26 Apr. 1904;
22 May 1905 (dir. Granville Barker, who played Marchbanks, with
Kate Rorke); Holborn Empire, 1 Mar. 1920 (dir. Bruce Winston; with
Sybil Thorndike, Lewis Casson, and Nicholas Hannen); Everyman
Th., Hampstead, 7 Feb. 1921 (dir. Edith Craig; des. Norman
Macdermott); Everyman Th., Hampstead, 24 July 1922 (dir. Douglas
Jefferies; with Ellen O'Malley, and Milton Rosmer as Marchbanks);
Everyman Th., 18 June 1923 (dir. Harold Scott; with Ellen O'Malley
and Alan Jeayes); Malvern Festival Th., 18 Aug. 1930 (dir. H. K.
Ayliff); Abbey Th., Dublin, 30 Sept. 1935; Globe Th., 10 Feb. 1937
(dir. Irene Hentschel; with Ann Harding, replaced by Diana Wynyard,
Nicholas Hannen as Morell, Stephen Hayward as Marchbanks,
Edward Chapman as Burgess, Athene Seyler as 'Prossy'); New
Bolton's Th., 12 Feb. 1951 (dir. Peter Cotes; with Joan Miller and
Andrew Cruickshank); Dundee Rep. Th. at Edinburgh Festival, 1959
(dir. Raymond Westwell); Piccadilly Th., London, 13 June 1960
(dir. Frank Hauser; des. Michael Richardson; with Dulcie Gray,
Michael Denison, and Jeremy Spenser); Roundabout Th., New York,
2 Feb. 1969 (dir. Gene Feist); Longacre Th., New York, 6 Apr. 1970
(dir. Laurence Carr; with Celeste Holm); Belgrade Th., Coventry,
31 Mar. 1976 (dir. Ed Thomason; des. Terry Parson; with Maggie
McCarthy); Albery Th., 23 June 1977 (dir. Michael Blakemore; with
Deborah Kerr, Denis Quilley, and Patrick Ryecart); King's Head
1987 (dir. Frank Hauser), rev. Arts Th., 12 Jan. 1988; Boulevard Th.,
Soho, 21 Sept. 1988 (dir. Rob Kennedy; with Julia Foster).

First published: in *Plays Pleasant and Unpleasant*, Vol. II, 1898.

Candida Morell, wife of the popular Christian Socialist,

Rev. James Mavor Morell, and daughter of the shifty yet genial contractor, Burgess, is idolized by the young poet Eugene Marchbanks from an aristocratic family, whom she has found sleeping rough and has taken under her wing. He criticizes James as both unappreciative and unworthy of his wife, and undermines his confidence in her love. Morell rises to the challenge to leave Candida alone with the poet, while he intoxicates the crowd with his words, as usual, at a public meeting. Then Candida takes control in an 'auction' scene, promising herself to whichever man puts in the higher bid. Eugene perceives that the appeal of weakness must weigh most with her motherly nature. A play full of teasingly ambiguous lights on character and relationships, which ends with Morell worshipping the angel in the house he cannot do without, and the poet repudiating domestic happiness to follow his higher destiny out into the darkness.

Candida, between you and me, is the Virgin Mother and nobody else.

> Shaw, to Ellen Terry, 6 Apr. 1896, *Collected Letters*, I, p. 623

It is quite a sentimental play, which I hope to find understood by women, if not by men.

> Shaw, *Collected Lettters*, I, p. 632

Candida is a pre-Raphaelite play. To distil the quintessential drama from pre-Raphaelitism, medieval or modern, it must be shown at its best in conflict with the first broken, nervous, stumbling attempts to formulate its own revolt against itself as it develops into something higher.

> Shaw, Preface to *Plays Pleasant and Unpleasant*, II, 1898

Candida is as unscrupulous as Siegfried: Morell himself sees that 'no law will bind her'. She seduces Eugene just exactly as far as it is worth her while to seduce him. She is a woman without character in the conventional sense. Without brains and strength of mind she would be a wretched slattern or voluptuary. ... Consider the poet. She makes a man of him finally by showing him his own strength. ...

> Shaw, to James Huneker, quoted in Huneker's *Iconoclasts*,
> New York: Charles Scribner's Sons, 1905, p. 254-5

Ibsen [in *A Doll's House*] made what was then an astounding innovation by first finishing his story completely, and then, instead of bringing down the curtain, ... making his characters sit down to discuss the play and draw the moral.

Now this is what happens in *Candida*. ... However, audiences do not trouble themselves about technical points; and the surprise in *Candida* 40 years ago was its turning the tables on *A Doll's House*. For though the cards are not packed against the husband as they were in Ibsen's play, and he is unquestionably a good fellow of high character and unselfish spirit, yet it is shown irresistibly that domestically he is the pet and the doll, and that it is his wife who runs the establishment and makes all his public triumphs possible.

Shaw, programme note for production at Globe Theatre, 10 Feb. 1937

When I began writing the part of the young poet, I had in mind De Quincey's account of his adolescence in his *Confessions*. I certainly never thought of myself as a model.

Shaw, *Evening Standard*, 28 Nov. 1944

Through no intrinsic fault of its own, Michael Blakemore's production of *Candida* confirms the impression that it is a consistently unsatisfactory play. ...

Fundamentally, the problem with the play is that it's peopled by three crashing bores. ... While the fresh temper of the Shavian intellect, radical and iconoclastic, bristles behind the play, nothing within it exceeds the strictly conventional. ...

Denis Quilley, taut, and wasting not a moment of impetus, plays the thankless role of Morell to the limit of the character's ordinariness. ... For me some of the best moments ... come when this bright impudent pup [Marchbanks] tells Morell of his inadequacies with such flashes of insight that Denis Quilley catches his breath in acknowledgment of the force of the point and [is] suddenly and believably jealous.

Ivan Howlett, *Plays and Players*, Aug. 1977, p. 25

Fortunately there are productions [of Shaw's plays] ... which blaze with a concern for the human beings who make the speeches; ... and what Frank Hauser makes us realize is the presence of abysses threatening to open beneath order and logic. ... The wife calmly holds a mirror of truth to the childish selfishness of the hyperbolic aesthete and her word-confident Christian Socialist husband which is anything but pleasant. ... What seems clear ... is that Shaw ... found in *Candida* a deeper resonance of his own obsession with words and a questioning of their ultimate value.

David Nice, Plays and Players, Feb. 1987, p. 27-8

You Never Can Tell

A comedy in four acts.
Written: 1895-96.
Copyright reading: Bijou Th., Bayswater, 23 Mar. 1898.
First (private) performance: Stage Society at Royalty Th., 26 Nov. 1899 (dir. James Welch, who also played the Waiter, with Yorke Stephens as Valentine, Margaret Halstan as Gloria).
First public production: Strand Th., 2 May 1900 (dir. James Welch, who played the Waiter).
First US (amateur) production: Chicago Musical College School of Acting at Studebaker Th., 24 Feb. 1903.
First US professional production: Garrick Th., New York, 9 Jan. 1905 (dir. Arnold Daly).
Revived: Royal Court Th., 2 May and 12 June 1905 (dir. Shaw and Granville Barker, who also played Valentine, with Louis Calvert as the Waiter, Nigel Playfair as Bohun, Tita Brand as Gloria), then 9 July 1906 (with Henry Ainley as Valentine, Lillah McCarthy as Gloria), and 11 Feb. and 1 Apr. 1907 (with Granville Barker as Valentine); Savoy Th., 16 Sept. 1907 (dir. Granville Barker; with Harcourt Williams as Valentine, Ellen O'Malley as Gloria, Nigel Playfair as Bohun); Garrick Th., 22 Nov. 1920 (dir. Louis Calvert, who also played the Waiter, with Francis Lister as Valentine, Viola Tree as Gloria, Lady Tree as Mrs. Clandon, Denys Blakelock as Philip); Everyman Th., 24 Jan. 1921 (dir. Edith Craig; with Nicholas Hannen as Valentine, Felix Aylmer as Bohun); Everyman Th., 14 May 1922 (dir. N. Macdermott; with Leslie Banks as Valentine, Gertrude Kingston as Mrs. Clandon, O.B. Clarence as the Waiter); Little Th., 26 Dec. 1927 (dir. Esmé Percy, who also played Valentine); Abbey Th., Dublin, 26 Dec. 1933; Malvern Festival Th., 27 July 1934 (dir. Herbert Prentice); Westminster Th., 3 May 1938 (dir. Michael MacOwan); Wyndham's Th., 3 Oct. 1947 (dir. Peter Ashmore; with Rosamund John as Gloria, Harcourt Williams as the Waiter, Ernest Thesiger as McComas), trans. to Criterion Th., 26 Apr. 1948; Birmingham Repertory Th., 27 Apr. 1955 (dir. Julian Amyes; des. Paul Shelving; with Redmond Phillips as the Waiter, Richard Pasco as Valentine); Pitlochry Festival Th., 26 Apr. 1958 (dir. Jordan Lawrence; des. Gillian Armitage); Gate

31

Th., Dublin, 28 Sept. 1964 (dir. Chloe Gibson; des. Alpho Reilly);
Haymarket Th., 12 Jan. 1966 (dir. Glen Byam Shaw; des. Motley;
with Ralph Richardson as the Waiter, Harry Andrews as Crampton);
Abbey Th., Dublin, 14 Apr. 1978 (dir. Patrick Mason; with
Cyril Cusack as the Waiter); Lyric Th., Hammersmith, 18 Oct. 1979
(dir. David Giles; with Paul Rogers as the Waiter, Sian Phillips as
Mrs. Clandon, Cheryl Campbell as Gloria); Brewhouse, Taunton,
20 Nov. 1984; Theatre Clwyd, Mold, 25 Sept. 1987 (dir. Toby
Robertson; des. Saul Radomsky; with Michael Hordern as the
Waiter), trans. Haymarket Th., London, 18 Dec. 1987 (Irene Worth
taking over as Mrs. Clandon, and Michael Denison as McComas).
First published: in *Plays Pleasant and Unpleasant*, Vol. II, 1898.

---

*A chance meeting, at a seaside dentist's, between an old man
and a pert young girl, who do not know themselves to be a long-
separated father and daughter, leads on to a general
reassembling of the broken family at a hotel lunch, in the
presence of Valentine the dentist, McComas the solicitor, and
the comic Waiter (traditionally the star role). Under her present
name of Mrs. Clandon, Crampton's estranged wife has become
a formidable feminist author and has brought up her beautiful
elder daughter, Gloria, in her own mould. Valentine's courtship
and intellectual seduction of Gloria culminates in their engagement: an embarcation on an uncertain future set against the
darker background of the previous generation's failure and
suffering. For the family is reconciled in a new understanding,
rather than reunited. The irrepressible twins, Dolly and Philip,
act as a comic chorus; the last act features an absurd judgment
by Bohun, QC, the Waiter's son; and emotional disturbances
and perplexities are waltzed away in a concluding carnival ball.*

... The tragedy will be between the father and the daughter.
Shaw, to Janet Achurch, 23 Dec. 1895,
Collected Letters, I, p. 583

It is rather difficult to determine how [*You Never Can Tell*] ought to be
acted. Realism and sheer fantasy are inextricably entangled in the
scheme of the play. ... All would seem quite right and proper, I should
have an impression of artistic unity, if Gloria and the dentist were played

as extravagantly as Mr. Bohun and the twins. ... And yet ... I am not quite sure that I would rather it were played in that way. The very worry and distraction caused by the serious acting were, in a sense, an addition to my delight in the play; for they kept me in mind of the author's peculiar temperament and attitude, of which the manifold contradictions are so infinitely more delightful, even when they make us very angry, than the smooth, intelligible consistency of you or me.

Max Beerbohm, *Saturday Review*, May 1900, reprinted. in
Around Theatres, second edition, p. 79

I wrote to [Shaw] suggesting he should let me see the play. He instantly undertook the management of our theatre to the extent of informing me that *Candida* would not suit us, but that he would write a new play for us. ... On the question of cutting, Mr. Shaw's attitude was nothing less than Satanic. ... He handed me the play, begged me to cut it freely, and then hypnotized me so that I could not collect my thoughts sufficiently to cut a single line. On the other hand, if I showed the least pleasure in a scene at rehearsal he at once cut it out on the ground that the play was too long.

Cyril Maude, *The Haymarket Theatre*, 1903, Chapter XVI
(on the abandoned production, ghost-written by Shaw)

It has always seemed merely a farce written round a waiter. It ought to be a very serious comedy, dancing gaily to a happy ending round the grim-earnest of Mrs. Clandon's marriage and her nineteenth-century George Eliotism.

Shaw, to Granville Barker, 6 Dec. 1904,
The Shaw-Barker Letters, p. 45

You Never Can Tell has proved one of the most popular of Mr. Shaw's plays, partly because its peculiar wit and high spirits communicate to the spectator's mind a kind of dancing freedom; and partly because the criticism in it upon social distinctions, the family, and the conventions of courtship, instead of being hurled in truculent harangues across the foot-lights, is conveyed indirectly during the course of the story — and, lastly, because the whole play is tinged with the serene resignation of the old waiter's gentle refrain. ... How beautifully Mr. Calvert played him! He gathered the teacups with the tenderness of a lady picking flowers in her garden; he proffered coats and parasols with a concern untouched by servility, but profoundly absurd; his voice was like oil on troubled waters; he was the personification of that sense of the importance of the

moment, which, emphasized, is the source of the most delicious irony.
Desmond MacCarthy, on revival of 2 May 1905,
reprinted in *Shaw*, Macgibbon and Kee, 1951, p. 37-8

The Devil's Disciple

Melodrama in three acts.
Written: 1896-97.
Copyright performance: Bijou Th., Bayswater, 17 Apr. 1897 (Shaw
 reading Anthony Anderson).
First production: Hermanus Bleecker Hall, Albany, New York, 1 Oct.
 1897, trans. Fifth Avenue Th., New York, 4 Oct. 1897
 (dir. Richard Mansfield, who played Richard Dudgeon).
First English production: Prince of Wales Th., Kennington, 26 Sept.
 1899 (dir. Murray Carson).
Revived: Coronet Th., Notting Hill Gate, 7 Sept. 1900 (dir. Shaw; with
 Forbes Robertson as Richard).
First production in German: Raimund Th., Vienna, 25 Feb. 1903.
First West End production: Savoy Th., 14 Oct. 1907 (dir. Shaw and
 Granville Barker, who also played General Burgoyne, with Matheson
 Lang as Richard), trans. to Queen's Th., 23 Nov. 1907 (with
 Granville Barker taking over as Richard).
Revived: Abbey Th., Dublin, 10 Feb. 1920 (dir. Lennox Robinson);
 Everyman Th., Hampstead, 24 Sept. 1924 (dir. Norman Macdermott;
 with Claude Rains); Festival Th., Cambridge, 30 Apr. 1928
 (dir. Terence Gray); Savoy Th., 2 Sept. 1930 (dir. Martin Harvey,
 who also played Richard, with Edmund Gwenn as Anderson and
 Margaret Webster as Judith); Old Vic Company at Buxton Festival,
 31 Aug. 1939, and Streatham Hill Th., 4 Oct. 1939, as part of tour
 (dir. Esmé Church, who also played Mrs. Dudgeon, with
 Robert Donat as Richard, Stewart Granger as Anderson, Sonia
 Dresdel as Judith); Old Vic Co., Golders Green Hippodrome,
 10 June 1940, trans. Piccadilly Th., 24 July 1940 (dir. Milton Rosmer,
 who also played Burgoyne, with Robert Donat as Richard, Roger
 Livesey as Anderson, Rosamund John as Judith); Gaiety Th., Dublin,
 1947 (with Cyril Cusack as Richard); Opera House, Manchester,
 20 Feb. 1956 (dir. Noel Willman; des. Anthony Holland; with
 Tyrone Power and Zena Walker), trans. Winter Garden Th., London,
 18 Nov. 1956; Yvonne Arnaud Th., Guildford, 14 Sept. 1965
 (dir. John Gibson; with Ian Bannen as Richard, Marius Goring as
 Burgoyne); Shaw Th., 5 July 1971 (dir. Michael Croft; with Tom Bell
 and Ray McAnally); RSC at Aldwych Th., 13 July 1976 (dir. Jack

Gold; with Tom Conti, T.P. McKenna, and Estelle Kohler);
Chichester Festival Th., 1978 (dir. Peter Dews; des. Sally Gardner;
with Ian Ogilvy, Brian Blessed, Mel Martin, and John Clements as
Burgoyne); Malvern Festival Th., Aug. 1981 (with Anthony Quayle
as Burgoyne).
First Published: in *Three Plays for Puritans*, Grant Richards, 1901.

*In Massachusetts during the War of Independence, the 'black
sheep' Richard Dudgeon attacks the narrow Puritan morality of
his mother and family, assembled to hear his dead father's will.
His romantic nature (and naturally Christian soul) traps him
into self-sacrifice, when English troops mistake him for the rebel
Minister, Anthony Anderson, upon finding him in the latter's
house with his young wife, Judith. At his trial Richard
matches his defiant humour against the cynical wit of General
Burgoyne. Anderson, discovering Richard's plight, acts in his
own true character of an energetic leader of men and rescues
the other on the brink of execution by bringing a force against
the English.*

Burgoyne is a gentleman; and that is the whole meaning of that part of
the play. It is not enough ... that Richard should be superior to religion
and morality as typified by his mother and his home, or to love as
typified by Judith. He must also be superior to gentility — that is, to the
whole ideal of modern society.

Shaw, to Ellen Terry, 13 Mar. 1897,
Collected Letters, I, p. 734

If the end of the second act produces the right effect, the sympathy goes
from the woman for her mistake about Anderson. ... It is extremely
difficult to hold up the horror of the court martial scene against Burgoyne and the rest, and to be made the butt of such cruel effect of his
'and that will do very nicely' when she takes refuge in agonized prayer
under the gallows (I understand that this has been totally missed, though
it is one of the most appalling things in the play). Nevertheless, these
scenes would be worth the labour they must cost, if you could fix the
audience's interest in you by striking home in the scene of the arrest.

Shaw, to Mrs. Richard Mansfield, 10 Dec. 1897,
Collected Letters, I, p. 830

The Devil's Disciple is a kind of existential comedy. Taking Binswanger's deduction of the three fundamental characteristics of human existence — 'first, man must design a world within space and time; second, he must establish himself within this world, which he can do through the third characteristic of acting and loving ...' — we can read Shaw's portrait of Dick Dudgeon as an attempt at an existential hero. ... There's a great danger that Dick may become a conventional matinee idol. ... It's only ... when, in classic Shavian style, he's loosed against a worthy adversary in the Rev. Anthony Anderson that his real heroism can catch fire. ...

Jack Gold's dazzling production balances Dick, Anderson and Burgoyne exactly. ... Tom Conti ... rides the part [of Dick] like it's a bronco in a rodeo. ... There are moments when he forces a chance into a racing certainty and somehow alienates whilst succeeding. ...

W. Stephen Gilbert, *Plays and Players*, Sept. 1976, p. 24

Caesar and Cleopatra

'A History' in four acts.

Written: 1898; new prologue, 1912.

Copyright performance: Mrs. Patrick Campbell's company at Theatre Royal, Newcastle-upon-Tyne, 15 Mar. 1899.

First American (amateur) production: student 'costume recital', Anna Morgan Studios for Art and Expression, Fine Arts Building, Chicago, 1 May 1901.

First professional production: Neues Theater, Berlin, 31 Mar. 1906 (prod. Max Reinhardt; dir. Hans Olden; with Gertrude Eysoldt), trans. Deutsches Theater, 15 June 1906.

First professional production in English: New Amsterdam Th., New York, 30 Oct. 1906 (dir. Shaw and Forbes Robertson, who also played Caesar), trans. Grand Th., Leeds, 16 Sept. 1907, trans. Savoy Th., London, 25 Nov. 1907 (with omission of Act III).

Revived: Theatre Royal, Drury Lane, 14 Apr. 1913 (dir. Shaw and Forbes Robertson, who played Caesar); Birmingham Repertory Th., 9 Apr. 1925 (dir. H. K. Ayliff; des. Paul Shelving; with Cedric Hardwicke and Gwen Frangçon Davies), trans. Kingsway Th., London, 1925; Abbey Th., Dublin, 24 Oct. 1927; (with both prologues); Malvern Festival Th., 24 Aug. 1929 (dir. Ayliff; des. Shelving; with Cedric Hardwicke and Dorothy Holmes-Gore); Old Vic Th., 19 Sept. 1932 (dir. Harcourt Wiliams; with Peggy Ashcroft); Opera House, Manchester, 24 Apr. 1951, trans. St. James's Th., 10 May 1951 (dir. Michael Benthall; des. Roger Furse; with

Laurence Olivier and Vivien Leigh); Birmingham Rep. Th.,
12 June 1956 (dir. Douglas Seale; des. Paul Shelving; with Geoffrey
Bayldon, Doreen Aris, and Albert Finney as Belzanor), trans.
Old Vic. Th., London, 30 July 1957; Duchess Th., 31 Aug. 1961
(dir. Waris Hussein; des. Ann Jasper); Chichester Festival Th.,
7 July 1971 (dir. Robin Phillips; with John Gielgud and Anna Calder-
Marshall); Palace Th., New York, 24 Feb. 1977 (dir. Ellis Rabb; with
Rex Harrison as Caesar); Theatre Clwyd, Oct. 1979; Shaw
Festival Th., Niagara-on-the-Lake, 1983.
Film version: with additional scenes and dialogue by Shaw, Rank Films,
1945 (dir. Gabriel Pascal; with Claude Rains and Vivien Leigh).
Musical Version: as *Her First Roman*, New York, 20 Oct. 1968.
First Published: in *Three Plays for Puritans*, 1901; new prologue first
published in French, trans. Augustin Hamon, 1926; in English, in
Collected Works, 1930.

---

*A five-act play which constantly recalls and counterpoints
Shakespeare's* Antony and Cleopatra, *though located at an
earlier point in the story of the Romans in Egypt. The original
Prologue enacts the alarm in the courtyard of Cleopatra's
palace as news of Caesar's approach arrives; the 1912 alternative is a monologue addressed to the audience by the God Ra
which fills in the historical context and, by the practice of
anachronism, insists on the modern relevance of the historical
play which follows. This opens with the chance meeting of Julius
Caesar with the young Cleopatra, hiding between the paws of a
sphinx and unaware of his identity. A judicious indulgence in
stage spectacle enables the epic of Caesar's Egyptian campaign
to be suggested as background to a drama of the education of
Cleopatra in the art of wise government. She grows into
maturity of judgment only to revert to the methods of conspiracy
and treachery, culminating in the assassination of Pothinus, her
young brother's political protector. The arrival of a relief army
averts disaster, and Caesar is able to depart peacefully, leaving
behind the loyal Rufio as Roman governor.*

He has come through experiment to the loose form of *Caesar and
Cleopatra* ... that large and variegated form wherein there is elbow-
room for all his irresponsible complexities.

Max Beerbohm, *Saturday Review*, 1 Feb. 1902

Caesar and Cleopatra is an attempt of mine to pay an instalment of the debt that all dramatists owe to the art of heroic acting. ... The demand now is for heroes ... who ... are heroic in the true human fashion: that is, touching the summits only at rare moments, and finding the proper level of all occasions, condescending with humour and good sense to the prosaic ones, as well as rising to the noble ones. ... Forbes Robertson ... is the classic actor of our day ... completely aloof in simplicity, dignity, grace and musical speech from the world of the motor car and the Carlton Hotel. ...

> Shaw, letter to *Play Pictorial*, No. 62, Oct. 1907

To see *Caesar and Cleopatra* is once again to regret Offenbach. None but the genius that set to lilting music the reckless wit of *Orphée aux Enfers* and *La Belle Hélène* could worthily 'score' this Shavian extravaganza. ... His tunes would fill up certain gaps, disguise certain *longeurs*, which were apparent last night. ... Perhaps ... Mr. Shaw's Caesar was not quite so solemn in intention as Mr. Forbes Robertson makes him in fact. Our admiration for Mr. Robertson's personality and talent is considerable and sincere. ... But he is not, no he is not, brimming over with fun.

> *The Times*, 26 Nov. 1907

For all its pretence of being a chronicle play, *Caesar and Cleopatra* is in fact a play of dialectic, in which what finally counts is the shape of sentences, the balance of phrases, the conversational interplay, the rhythm of statement and counterstatement, the orchestration of the dialogue. All this is muffled [at the St. James's] by the heavy blanket of overproduction: too much movement, too many extras, too much noise.

> T. C. Worsley, *The New Statesman*,
> reprinted in *The Fugitive Art*, John Lehmann, 1952, p. 225

Roger Furse designed some splendid scenery, a colossal Sphinx between whose paws the kittenish Cleopatra of Shaw's play was discovered on the rising of the curtain; and a very fine arrangement of Roman pillars leaping superbly out of the burning desert sands. ... Robert Helpmann was an excellent Apollodorus, and he took a flying leap into the sea off the African battlements that will be long remembered. ... Sir Laurence's Caesar was much admired; and it was admirable. ... In his present phase of development he compasses the wise man who has never known passion better than the ageing roué who is being ruined by it.

> Harold Hobson, *The Theatre Now*, 1954, p. 151-2

At Chichester, the season ... has brought us a thoroughly entertaining revival of Shaw's Shakespearian mockery, *Caesar and Cleopatra*. ... Set in a pure white children's playroom, ... it affords the glorious sight of Sir John Gielgud on a slide and Anna Calder-Marshall on a bouncing ball. But ... the play suffers surprisingly little from Mr. Phillips's desperate search for laughs, and it may well need at least some of the help he offers along the way. Above all the production is true to its own eccentric self and has the courage of its interpretation ...

> Sheridan Morley, *Review Copies*, Robson Books, 1974, p. 85

Captain Brassbound's Conversion

Written: 1899.

Copyright reading: Court Th., Liverpool; 10 Oct. 1899 (with Ellen Terry and Laurence Irving).

First (private) performances: Stage Society at Strand Th., 16 Dec. 1900, and Criterion Th., 20 Dec. 1900 (dir. Charles Charrington; with Janet Achurch, Laurence Irving, and Granville Barker as Kearney).

First public production: Queen's Th., Manchester, 12 May 1902 (dir. Charles Charrrington; with Janet Achurch).

Revived: Court Th., 20 Mar. 1906 (dir. Shaw and Granville Barker; with Ellen Terry), also twelve-week run commencing 16 Apr. 1906; Empire Th., New York, 28 Jan. 1907 (prod. Charles Frohman); Little Th., 15 Oct. 1912 (dir. Shaw; with Gertrude Kingston); Everyman Th., 15 Oct. 1912 (dir. Tristan Rawson; with Malcolm Morley); Lyric Th., Hammersmith, 13 Oct. 1948 (dir. John Counsell; with Flora Robson); King's Th., Glasgow, 12 Mar. 1951, trans. Old Vic Th., 17 Apr. 1951 (dir. Hugh Hunt; with Ursula Jeans and Roger Livesey); Th. Royal, Bristol, 7 Sept. 1958 (dir. Paul Lee; with Joan Heal, Denis Quilley as Brassbound, Emrys James as Drinkwater, Peter Jeffrey as Hallam); Theatre Workshop, Th. Royal, Stratford, 27 Nov. 1960 (dir. John Bury; with Avis Bunage); Oxford Playhouse, 22 Nov. 1965 (dir. Anthony Besch; with Barbara Jefford); Cambridge Th., 18 Feb. 1971 (dir. Frith Banbury; with Ingrid Bergman and Joss Ackland), trans. Ethel Barrymore Th., New York, 17 Apr. 1972 (dir. Stephen Poster; with Ingrid Bergman and Pernel Roberts); Haymarket Th., 10 June 1982 (dir. Frank Hauser; with Penelope Keith, John Turner, and Michael Denison as Hallam).

First Published: in *Three Plays for Puritans*, 1901.

Judge Hallam, with his intrepid sister-in-law Lady Cicely Wayneflete, accepts an escort of villains and ne'er-do-wells commanded by the mysterious Captain Brassbound, for a journey to the interior of Morocco. He leads them into a trap, and the desert adventure plot is complicated with a revenge-melodrama when the Captain reveals himself as the Judge's wronged nephew. Lady Cicely, who manages men by treating them as children, persuades Brassbound of the absurdity of his heroic pose. She is equally critical of the spirit of vengeance institutionalized in the justice Hallam represents. When the turns of the adventure deliver all the westerners into the hands of the Captain of an American ship, Brassbound is brought before a court of inquiry. Lady Cicely, Portia-like, plays a barrister's role, but to the effect that no-one is sentenced. A conventional happy ending threatens, but is averted in favour of a genuinely more satisfactory resolution.

... The steamer calls at Tangier. I want to see a Moorish town, as the *Witch of Atlas* [*original title*] scene is laid in Mogador, except the second act, which is in the mountains. ... The *Witch of Atlas* ought to be done in a small theatre to get the best effect out of it.

Shaw, to Ellen Terry, 14 July 1899,
Ellen Terry and Bernard Shaw: a Correspondence, 1931

Ellen [Terry] herself was magnificent. She had actually become Lady Cicely. She no longer hampers herself as she did at the Court by trying to remember my lines: she simply lives through Lady Cicely's adventures and says whatever comes into her head, which by the way is now much better than what I wrote.

Shaw, to Forbes Robertson, *The Shaw-Barker Letters*, p. 61

One of the most curiously neglected of Bernard Shaw's plays pleasant, provides ... an admirably serviceable vehicle for the stellar theatrical talents of Ingrid Bergman. ... Miss Bergman's reading of the part may be a trifle erratic, missing some of the subtleties of Shaw's language, but the radiance of her presence is ample compensation. ... Shaw has set his play in Morocco, though his understanding of that country seems to have been as hazy as Louis B. Mayer's concept of Biblical Egypt. His plot ... is padded and chorused by an eccentric band of Peter Pannish sailors led by Kenneth Williams. ... But ... only two performances linger in the memory: John Robinson's severely upright Hallam and of course Miss Bergman's Cicely, whom she plays at full pelt as the dauntless, unpredictable, fearless, bossy, gracious, meddlesome, cheerful lady that Shaw undoubtedly intended.

Sheridan Morley, *Review Copies*, p. 67-8

The Admirable Bashville
or Constancy Unrewarded

Blank-verse skit in three acts (or two tableaux containing four scenes), derived from Shaw's novel, *Cashel Byron's Profession*.

Written: 1901.

First production: by amateurs, Pharos Club, Covent Garden, 4 Dec. 1902 (dir. Norreys Connell).

First professional production: Stage Society at Imperial Th., 7 and 8 June 1903 (dir. Shaw and Granville Barker).

First public production: Th. Royal, Manchester, 22 Sept. 1905 (dir. Harold V. Neilson).

First public production in London: Matinee Theatre at His Majesty's Th., 26 Jan. 1909 (dir. Shaw; with Ben Webster, Henry Ainley, Marie Löhr, Rosina Filippi).

First US production: Little Th., Philadelphia, 8 Feb. 1915.

Revived: Liverpool Playhouse, 1928 (dir. William Armstrong); Malvern Festival Th., 18 Aug. 1930 (dir. H. K. Ayliff; des. Paul Shelving; with Gwen Ffrangçon-Davies); Abbey Th., Dublin, 8 June 1931; Old Vic Th., 13 Feb. 1933 (dir. Harcourt Wlliams; with Roger Livesey); Arts Th., 26 Apr. 1951 (dir. Judith Furse; with John Slater, Maurice Denham, Brenda Bruce, Vivienne Bennett).

Musical version: as *Bashville*, Open Air Th., Regent's Park, 2 Aug. 1983 (adaptation and lyrics by Benny Green; music by Dennis King; dir. David William).

First published: in *Cashel Byron's Profession*, Grant Richards, 1901.

A burlesque in 'rigmarole' blank verse, in which the well-born Lydia falls in love with the boxer Cashel Byron, who worships her beauty as she adores his strength. After encounters with the footman Bashville, who secretly adores Lydia himself, and with a Zulu tribe watching his prize fight with a fellow-pugilist named Paradise, Cashel finds himself pursued by the police,

41

*and also by his own mother — who, revealing her son's
aristocratic origins at an opportune moment, finds herself a
noble husband at the same time as removing the obstacle to
Cashel's marriage to Lydia.*

Provided you run *Bashville* through without intervals, like a pantomime,
you had better do it your own way. My way was the Elizabethan Stage
way, with canvases making an inner stage, and the wings on the outer
stage. Two beefeaters carried on placards denoting the scenes. ... There
were all sorts of tomfooleries. ...

I am sorry to have to add that as the British public cannot understand
a literary joke, the play simply bewilders the audience, except when they
take the big speeches seriously and applaud them, especially Cashel's
'repudiation' of gentility. ...

Shaw, to William Armstrong, 26 Sept. 1928

Man and Superman

'A Comedy and a Philosophy' in four acts (of which Act III is
    commonly omitted, or Act III, Scene ii, played separately under title,
    Don Juan in Hell).
Written: 1901-03.
First (private) performances: without Act III, Stage Society at Court
    Th., 21 May 1905 (dir. Shaw; with Granville Barker and Lillah
    McCarthy).
First public performance: Vedrenne-Barker company, Court Th.,
    23 May 1905 (as produced for Stage Society, with same cast).
First production of Don Juan in Hell: Vedrenne-Barker company, Court
    Th., 4 June 1907 (dir. Shaw and Granville Barker; with Robert
    Loraine as Juan, and Lillah McCarthy).
First US production: without Act III, Hudson Th., New York, 5 Sept.
    1905 (presented by Charles Dillingham).
Revived without Act III: Vedrenne-Barker company, Court Th., 23 Oct.
    1905, 29 Oct. 1906, and 27 May 1907 (dir. Granville Barker);
    Criterion Th., 28 Sept. 1911 (dir. Robert Loraine, who played Tanner,
    with Pauline Chase); Criterion Th., 8 Apr. 1912 (dir. Robert Loraine,
    who played Tanner, with Hilda Bruce-Potter); Abbey Th., Dublin,
    26 Feb. 1917; Everyman Th., 23 May 1921 (dir. Edith Craig;
    des. Norman Macdermott; with Nicholas Hannen and Muriel Pratt);
    Kingsway Th., 10 Feb. 1927 (dir. Esmé Percy, who played Tanner,

with Gwen Ffrangçon-Davies); Little Th., 20 Jan. 1928 (dir. Esmé
Percy, who played Tanner, with Margot Drake); Court Th.,
6 Jan. 1930 (dir. Esmé Percy, who played Tanner, with Margot
Drake); Court Th., 6 Jan. 1930 (dir. Esmé Percy, who played Tanner,
with Rosalind Fuller); Court Th., 3 Mar. 1930 (dir. Esmé Percy; with
Alice Darch); Cambridge Th., 12 Aug. 1935 (dir. Esmé Percy; with
Margaret Rawlings); Old Vic Th., 21 Nov. 1938 (dir. Lewis Casson;
des. Ruth Keating; with Anthony Quayle and Valerie Tudor);
Birmingham Th., 14 Aug. 1945 (dir. Peter Brook; des. Paul
Shelving); King's Th., Hammersmith, 9 Apr. 1946 (dir. Lewis
Casson; des. Peter Goffin; with Basil C. Langton and Ann Casson);
Embassy Th., 17 May 1949 (dir. Terence O'Brien, who played
Tanner, with Ruth Spalding); New Th., 14 Feb. 1951 (dir. John
Clements, who played Tanner; des. Laurence Irving and Elizabeth
Haffenden; with Kay Hammond as Ann); King's Th., Glasgow,
29 Feb. 1951; Gate Th., Dublin, 1951 (dir. Dan O'Connell);
Th. Royal, Bristol, 11 Mar. 1968 (Bristol Old Vic Co. dir. John
Moody; des. Patrick Robertson and Rosemary Verco; with Peter
O'Toole); Malvern Festival Th., Aug. 1977 (with Richard Pasco and
Susan Hampshire); Birmingham Rep. Th., 27 Sept. 1982 (dir. Patrick
Dromgoole; with Peter O'Toole), trans. Haymarket Th., London,
16 Nov. 1982.

Don Juan in Hell *revived alone:* Arts Th., 24 Mar. 1943, 3 July 1946,
and 8 Sept. 1952 (dir. Alec Clunes, who played Juan, with otherwise
different casts); Coronet Th., Los Angeles, July 1947, then tour of 52
cities across USA, arriving Carnegie Hall, New York, 22 Oct. 1951
(platform recital in evening dress, dir. Charles Laughton, who also
read the Devil, with Charles Boyer, Agnes Moorehead, and Sir Cedric
Hardwicke), brought to Palace Th., Manchester, 18 June 1951 (dir.
Paul Gregory, with original cast).

First production of play in its entirety: Lyceum Th., Edinburgh, 11 June
1915 (dir. Esmé Percy, who played Tanner).

First London production of play in its entirety: Regent Th., King's
Cross, 23 Oct. 1925 (dir. Esmé Percy, who played Tanner, with
Valerie Richards).

Revived in its entirety: Little Th.; 27 Jan. 1928 (dir. Esmé Percy; with
Francis L. Sullivan as Mendoza and the Devil), trans. Garrick Th., 13
Feb. 1928; Court Th., 21 Jan. 1930 (dir. Esmé Percy; with Rosalinde
Fuller, and Wilfrid Lawson as Mendoza and the Devil); Embassy Th.,
2 Dec. 1937 (dir. Esmé Percy; with Margaret Rawlings), and at
Cambridge Th., 23 Aug. 1935; Old Vic, 21 Nov. 1938 (dir. Lewis
Casson; with Anthony Quayle); King's Th., Hammersmith,
9 Apr. 1946 (dir. Lewis Casson; with Basil C. Langton and Ann
Casson); Prince's Th., 2 June 1951 (dir. John Clements and Esmé

Percy; with Clements as Tanner, Kay Hammond as Ann); New Arts
Th., 23 Nov. 1965 (dir. Philip Wiseman; with Alan Badel, Sian
Phillips and Marie Löhr), trans. Vaudeville Th., 6 Jan. 1966; RSC at
Savoy Th., 16 Aug. 1977 (dir. Clifford Williams; with Richard Pasco,
Susan Hampshire); National Th. at Olivier, 22 Jan. 1981
(dir. Christopher Morahan; des. Ralph Koltai; with Daniel Massey,
Penelope Wilton, and Michael Bryant).
First published: London: Constable, 1903.

---

*The wealthy socialist, Jack Tanner, is appointed guardian of
Ann Whitfield and her sister, under their father's will. He
demonstrates his blind idealism by misjudging the character and
situation of Ann's friend Violet; and it takes his chauffeur to
make his realise that Ann intends to marry* him *and not the
chivalrous Octavius. His attempt to run away to Spain is foiled
by Ann's arrangement to make it a joint tour with family and
friends. In Act III, Jack in the Sierra dreams that he is Don
Juan, arguing in Hell with the Devil and expounding the theory
of creative evolution to him, Donna Anna, and the Commenda-
tore (from the Don Juan legend). This prepares him to accept
fatalistically his capture by Ann.*

When I venture to say that Mr. Shaw is no dramatist I do not mean that
he fails to interest and stimulate and amuse us in the theatre. Many of us
find him more entertaining than any other living writer for the stage. ...
There is waste, because Mr. Shaw neglects, or more probably is impo-
tent to fulfil, what Pater calls the responsibility of the artist to his
material. ... We want a play that shall be a vehicle for the Shavian
philosophy and the Shavian talent and, at the same time, a perfect
play. ... We certainly do not get it in *Man and Superman*. ... The action-
plot is well-nigh meaningless without the key of the idea-plot; ... and ...
it is because of this parasitic nature of the action-plot, because of its
weakness, its haphazardness, its unnaturalness, considered as a 'thing in
itself', that one finds the play as a play unsatisfying.

> A. B. Walkley, *Times Literary Supplement*, 26 May 1905;
> reprinted in *Drama and Life*, Methuen, 1907, p. 225-6

To put a boy of this age [*Peter Brook at twenty*] in charge of such a terror as *Man and Superman*, could anybody, even at the Rep, call this a reasonable risk? ... The players accepted Brook and responded to his precisely formed ideas, taking the text slower than usual, thinking carefully about it, keeping the arguments in flow, dodging nothing. ... [The] performance was lucidity itself, and if Scofield's Tanner had to depend now and then upon the charm that can be a bloom on Shavian actors, ... it was clear that he and Brook understood each other.

J. C. Trewin, *Peter Brook*, Macdonald, 1971,
p. 20 (on 1945 production)

Shaw's comedies are technically brilliant. Indeed, they are practically foolproof, though the amount of laughter they generate depends on the skill of producer and actor. ... Not to beat about the bush, Miss Hammond is simply impossible in Shaw. Her particular trick of speech, by which in modern comedy she gets all her characteristic effects, is a slow, over-articulated drawl, insinuating an innuendo. For most of Shaw an opposite technique is required. ... She completely holds things up. Even her listening — and about half the Shavian actor's skill is spent on listening — ... is twenty times too gradual, as she moves her great round eyes in a slow arc ...

T. C. Worsley, *The Fugitive Art*, John Lehmann, 1952, p. 206

Shaw ... claimed that Jack Tanner ... was based on the socialist H. M. Hyndman, but his contemporaries knew better. The play isn't just a satiric self-portrait. ... Tanner ... is acute as well as myopic. ...

The trouble is that Creative Evolution, with its emphasis on the intellect and will, its faith in the genius leader, ... now seems to tell us more about Shaw than the universe. ... *Man and Superman* itself tends to mock the intellectual pretensions of *Don Juan*, demonstrating that only in an imaginary world, free from the pressures of reality, can Tanner's theory survive intact. ...

The interpolation of *Don Juan* produces a richer, more complex play, one which leaves us with conflicting feelings ...

Benedict Nightingale, *New Statesman*, 30 Jan. 1981, p. 23

Strain, yes; wasted effort, no. *Man and Superman* may be brilliantly self-sufficient in the usual three-act version, but the restoration of the missing act vitally readjusts the balance of the surrounding play. ... The leading actor has two roles which throw each other into sharp relief. Down in Hell, Daniel Massey returns to the vein of steely melancholy ... combined with a superb command of Shaw's tidally surging paragraphs, fully operatic, except that the sense always comes before the music.

[As] Tanner, by contrast ... the words come tumbling out, but what they express for the most part is sheer panic.

Irving Wardle, The Times, 23 Jan. 1981

I wondered ... whether an adventurous director might not now give Shaw the 'modern dress' treatment. In this case Tanner would have to be a more serious revolutionary, even though ultimately harmless. I imagined the part played by Jonathan Pryce with Mr. Paul Foot in mind. Ann would have to be a liberated woman of the kind we might recognize today. The 'hell' sequence would have to be played with an ominous sense of the danger of irrationality in politics — a topical enough matter at a time when liberal democracy is in some disrepute. Hegel is coming back into fashion; and there is a growing yearning for a new religion. I suspect, however, that Shaw has become irrevocably dated and that Christopher Morahan was wise to go for a period piece production in the impeccably Shavian manner.

Peter Jenkins, The Spectator, 31 Jan. 1981

O'Toole plays Tanner like a man drunk with rhetoric. ... It is a dangerous performance, for its élan and speed might shatter the play. But on the contrary it breathes into it the breath of life. ... He ... fills the audience with an excitement which I have rarely known in a London theatre.

Harold Hobson, Times Literary Supplement, 3 Dec. 1982

Don Juan in Hell

I wanted Donna-Anna to be a type of exaggerated femininity, in an Infanta hoop and a perfect collection of Virgins, Holy Hearts, and 'Memento Moris' in nests of lace, with a white napkin and black gloves; Don Juan to be a creature of silver and purple, also in a sort of half mourning; and the Commandatore to be in Roman armour, buskins, ruffs, and a sash, in a true mock-heroic get-up, with a touch of comedy. This frightened Shaw; he wanted nothing that would take from the dignity of the figure, the comedy should be in the words. ...

Charles Ricketts, Self-Portrait, ed. Cecil Lewis, p. 128-9

Mr. Clunes has enormous respect for his author's intentions; his production, accordingly, is wholeheartedly egocentric. The action is a debate between Don Juan, his ex-mistress Donna Anna, her father, and the Devil about the rival merits of Heaven and Hell; and the trouble with it is that all Shaw's artillery is on the side of the angels. Mr. Clunes seizes on this hint to turn the play into *Saint Juan*. He anoints the part with an overwhelming complacency, wreathed in a halo of weary smiles, and a pointblank refusal to give the Devil his due. David Bird's Satan, all fuss and bluster, is allowed no authority at all: he has only to open his mouth for Mr. Clunes to sigh, shrug, and grin at him as at a truant child. And if he patronizes the Devil, Mr. Clunes positively *dandles* the other two. All this is done with a silken, non-creasing technical assurance: and the play emerges as just the outrageously lop-sided affair Shaw meant it to be. Don Juan is first, and hell nowhere.

Kenneth Tynan, *Curtains*, Longmans, 1961, p. 29-30

We wanted not necessarily the best actors, but the best voices in America. ... Boyer [Don Juan] is a master of the *tirade* and as such is invaluable in our play — not every actor can handle that difficult form of dramatic speech.

Charles Laughton, quoted by Kurt Singer,
in *The Laughton Story*, Robert Hale, 1954, p. 216

We shoot lines at each other in an unexpected way — just as a tennis player will shoot a ball at you and you get the thrill of making the right return. It must not be assumed that we try to defeat one another — it is just the fun of inventing new readings. ... Never for an instant have we failed to be stimulated in performing this play, although it involves the greatest strain that actors can be put to — which is listening to each other.

Sir Cedric Hardwicke, quoted in *The Laughton Story*, p. 222-3

Laughton's Satan is consummately realistic and consummately intelligent. ... Moonfaced, stout, wearing a respectable tuxedo, with reading-glasses on his nose. ... At the beginning he is almost lovable ... shy, slow of speech, diffident. He keeps his head bent so low that his chin brushes his shirt collar. He has a funny little smile and an impish little giggle. Surely there's no harm in the fellow, everyone thinks. But after a while he gains courage, becomes bolder. Before the audience knows it he is a full-fledged Devil thundering forth the wonderful lines Shaw wrote for him:

'Have you walked up and down lately? I have; and I have examined man's wonderful inventions ... the most destructive of all the destroyers.'

Kurt Singer, *The Laughton Story*, p. 219-21

John Bull's Other Island

A play in four acts.
Written: 1904.
First production: Vedrenne-Barker company, Court Th., 1 Nov. 1904 (dir. Shaw and Granville Barker; with Louis Calvert, J. L. Shine as Larry, Granville Barker as Keegan).
First US production: Garrick Th., New York, 10 Oct. 1905 (dir. Arnold Daly).
Revived: Vedrenne-Barker company, Court Th., 7 Feb. 1905 (with Louis Calvert, C. M. Hallard, Granville Barker); Kingsway Th., 26 Dec. 1912 (dir. Granville Barker; with Louis Calvert, Harcourt Williams, William Poel); Abbey Th., Dublin, 26 Sept. 1916, and annual revivals until 1931 (usually with Barry Fitzgerald as Broadbent, F. J. McCormick as Doyle); Court Th., 9 Sept. 1921 (dir. Allan Wade); 'Q' Th., 12 Dec. 1938 (dir. George Bancroft; with Raymond Lovell and Esmé Percy); Embassy Th., Swiss Cottage, 2 Dec. 1947 (Dublin Gate Th. company, dir. Hilton Edwards, who played Broadbent, with Michael MacLiammoir as Larry); Abbey Th., Dublin, 10 Mar. 1969; Mermaid Th., 13 May 1971 (dir. Alan Strachan; with Christopher Benjamin and Edward Petherbridge); Greenwich Th., 29 May 1980 (dir. Alan Strachan); Irish Th. Co., 1980 (dir. Patrick Mason; with Cyril Cusack as Keegan).
First published: in *John Bull's Other Island and Major Barbara*, New York: Brentano's, 1907; London: Constable, 1907.

The business partners, Broadbent, an ebullient English Liberal, and the embittered Doyle, visit Doyle's family in Ireland. Broadbent, full of romantic ideas of the country, promptly falls in love with Nora and proposes marriage. Hysterically amused at his foolishness, the locals adopt him as their parliamentary candidate. Keegan, the ex-priest, denounces the self-interested materialism which is the Doyle-Broadbent response to all Ireland's ills.

I thought in reading the first act that you had forgotten Ireland but I found in the other acts that [it] is the only subject on which you are entirely serious. ... You have said things in this play which are entirely true about Ireland, things which nobody has ever said before, and these are the very things that are most part of the action. It astonishes me that you should have been so long in London and yet have remembered so much. ... Synge ... thinks that 'it will hold a Dublin audience, and at times move them if even tolerably played'. He thinks however you should cut the grasshopper, and a scene which I cannot recall, but which he describes as 'the Handy Andy-like scene about carrying the goose' and some of the Englishman's talk about Free Trade, Tariffs, etc. ... You will see by Fay's letter that he is nervous about being able to cast it. I imagine the Englishman will give us most difficulty, but it will all be difficult.

W. B. Yeats, letter to Shaw, 5 Oct. 1904, in *Letters*, ed. A. Wade

The author has written a formless piece of excellent fooling, with just an undercurrent of seriousness. ... But behind all the wit and the broad humour I caught a glimpse of a Bernard Shaw in the white heat of seriousness. It was very pretty rapier work — the accomplishment of a master — but the rapier had no buttons. ... [The] slight love story, which at first seemed so vague and unnecessary that one rather resented it, gives, perhaps, the clue to Mr. Shaw's real meaning — a pessimistic meaning. ... Mr. Shaw employed symbolism with the tact and delicacy of a poet. He has even given a version of the awakening of Brunnhilde by Siegfried. But what a Siegfried!

E. A. Baughan, *Daily News*, 2 Nov. 1904

Broadbent is a full-length portrait, minutely finished ... certainly Mr. Shaw's masterpiece of observation and of satire. The satire is the more deadly by reason of (what Broadbent would call) the 'conspicuous fairness' with which it is accomplished. Mr. Shaw sees all Broadbent's good points, and lays stress on everything that is not absurd in him. The tone is always kindly, even affectionate. We are quite sure that justice is being done. ... No Englishman could deny the truth of Broadbent. Indeed, no thoroughbred Englishman would wish to deny the truth of Broadbent. That is the cream of the joke.

Max Beerbohm, *Saturday Review*, 12 Nov. 1904

Nigel [Playfair] ... is a perfect godsend. If you can't cure him, with one word, of making Broadbent a CAD, I can; but neither you nor I can cure

Louis [Calvert] of making him a hippopotamus and revolting people who cannot melt over a baby of that species. Nigel ... has to be taught the proper platform intonations for the political windbaggery ... to be shown two or three touches in the second love scene. ... Of course, it will not be Calvert, but then in the nature of things the future history of [*John Bull's Other Island*] must be a history of broadly comic Broadbents, and not happy accidents like Calvert's personality. ... You hate the thing because it is a garish projection of an overemphasized personality; but it draws and pays. And my plays are built to stand that sort of thing.

Shaw, to Granville Barker, 20 July 1907,
in *Shaw-Barker Letters*, p. 96

Shaw's place in the heart of the British playgoer is distinctly insecure. Even with each star-studded limited season down Shaftesbury Avenue comes a suspicion ... that the man's credibility, like Harold Wilson's, will fade in direct proportion to the amount of public scrutiny accorded his work. ... Suddenly we are confronted with a virtually unknown work, last performed in London in 1947. ... The discovery is remarkable, not because of the play's highly topical exposure of English interference in Ireland, but because the vitality and comic bravura of the writing is joyously equal to anything else that Shaw wrote. Shaw was as patriotic about Ireland as he was about England, but he was insistent that Home Rule was any nation's lawful right. ... He admits the inevitability of some attempt at governmental efficiency. There is a deep sadness at the root of this admission, a sadness impressively caught in Alan Strachan's production. ... Herein lies the power of the comedy: the steely satire of the piece is tempered by a serious acknowledgment of the political problems. ...

To get laughs with consistent ease for over three hours in the portrayal of what is essentially a rather two-dimensional character is a tribute to both Shaw's writing and [Christopher] Benjamin's resourcefulness ...

The profound melancholy of the play's statement is so untypically Shavian that the temptation to gild the lily must be resisted in order to make the play work in its more obviously comic aspects. This Strachan fully achieves, with the help of a setting by Bernard Culshaw. ... I have never seen the Mermaid's wide proscenium put to better use and the crackling debate of Act III benefits particularly from this physical asset.

Michael Coveney, *Plays and Players*, July 1971, p. 47

How He Lied to Her Husband

Comedy in one act.

Written: 1904.

First US production: Berkeley Lyceum, New York, 26 Sept. 1904
(dir. and acted Arnold Daly).

First production in England: Vedrenne-Barker company, Court Th.,
28 Feb. 1905 (dir. and played Granville Barker, with Gertrude
Kingston).

Revived: St. James's Th., 21 Mar. 1905, and Savoy Th., 8 May 1905
(dir. Granville Barker, with cast from Court Th.); in music hall bill,
Palace Th., 4 Dec. 1911 (dir. and played Harcourt Williams; with
Margaret Halstan); Everyman Th., Hampstead, 14 Mar. 1921
(dir. Edith Craig; des. Norman Macdermott; with Harold Scott,
Inez Cameron, and Felix Aylmer); Everyman Th., 27 Aug. 1924
(dir. Norman Macdermott; with Harold Scott, Clare Harris, and Felix
Aylmer); Arts Th., 1951 (dir. Stephen Murray; with Maurice Denham
and Brenda Bruce); Fortune Th., 26 Jan. 1970 (dir. Michael Denison;
des. Motley; with Clive Francis, June Barry, Robert Flemyng);
Bellerby Th., Guildford, 1980; Redgrave Th., Farnham, 24 May 1983.

Film: British International Pictures, 1930.

First published: in German, 1906; in English, in *John Bull's Other
Island and Major Barbara*, New York: Brentano's, 1907; London:
Constable, 1907.

---

*A young poet denies addressing his romantic poems to a
married woman, in order to protect her from discovery by her
husband. The latter's unexpected response indicates that
triangular relationships may be more complex affairs than is
generally realized.*

The drama of Mr. Bernard Shaw made its first appearance on the variety
stage last night. ... [T]his joke at the expense of *Candida* is a pure
delight. The farcical element in it — those amateurish fisticuffs between
husband and lover — is a genuine part of the play, which Mr. Shaw's
farce not always is. And think what they were fighting about! Because
Mr. Bombas thought Mr. Apjohn was not in love with Mrs. Bompas! ...
The whole thing is delicious, whether you bother about *Candida* or not,
and delicious it proved to be to an audience which seemed to want it all
over again.

The Times, 5 Dec. 1911

51

Major Barbara

A discussion in three acts.

Written: 1905.

First production: Vedrenne-Barker company, Court Th., 28 Nov. 1905 (dir. Shaw and Granville Barker; with Annie Russell, Louis Calvert, Granville Barker).

First US production: Playhouse Th., New York, 9 Dec. 1915 (with Grace George).

Revived: Court Th., 1 Jan. 1906 (dir. Granville Barker); Everyman Th., Hampstead, 18 Apr. 1921 (dir. Edith Craig; des. Norman Macdermott, with Dorothy Massingham, Nicholas Hannen, Felix Aylmer); Everyman Th., 27 Aug. 1923 (dir. Norman Macdermott; with Dorothy Massingham, Alan Jeayes, Felix Aylmer); Wyndham's Th., 5 Mar. 1929 (dir. Lewis Casson and Charles Macdona; with Sybil Thorndike, Balliol Holloway, Lewis Casson, and Gordon Harker as Bill Walker); Old Vic Th., 4 Mar. 1935 (dir. Henry Cass; with Mary Newcombe, Cecil Trouncer, Maurice Evans); Westminster Th., 20 Dec. 1939 (dir. John Fernald; with Catherine Lacey, Stephen Murray, Robert Harris); Lyric Th., Hammersmith, Sept. 1942 (dir. Reginald Long; with Ellen Pollock); Arts Th., 30 Mar. 1948 (dir. Peter Glenville; with Barbara Lott); Bedford Th., Camden Town, 13 June 1949 (dir. Douglas Seale); Th. Royal, Bristol, 26 June 1956 (dir. John Moody; des. Patrick Robertson; with Moira Shearer, Joseph O'Conor as Undershaft, Derek Godfrey as Cusins, Marie Burke, Alan Dobie, Edward Hardwick, and Peter O'Tooole as Peter Shirley), trans. Old Vic Th., London, 16 July 1956; Martin Beck Th., New York, 30 Oct. 1956 (dir. Charles Laughton, who also played Undershaft, with Glynis Johns, Cornelia Otis Skinner, and Eli Wallach as Bill Walker); Royal Court Th., 28 Aug. 1958 (dir George Devine; des. Motley; with Joan Plowright, Alan Webb, Paul Daneman, Vanessa Redgrave); RSC at Aldwych Th., 19 Oct. 1970 (dir. Clifford Williams; des. Ralph Koltai; with Judi Dench, Brewster Mason, Richard Pasco); Birmingham Rep. Th., 14 Apr. 1980 (dir. Peter Farago); National Th. at Lyttelton, 27 Oct. 1982 (dir. Peter Gill; with Penelope Wilton, Brewster Mason, and Sian Phillips as Lady Britomart).

Film: with additional scenes and dialogue by Shaw, 1940-41 (dir. Gabriel Pascal; with Wendy Hiller, Robert Morley, Rex Harrison, and Robert Newton as Bill Walker), *published:* Penguin Books, 1946.

First published: in *John Bull's Island and Major Barbara*, New York: Brentano's, 1907; London: Constable, 1907.

Lady Britomart summons her estranged husband, Andrew Undershaft, a millionaire armaments manufacturer, to provide for the future of their grown-up children. This initiates a trial of strength between the arms merchant, his salvationist daughter Barbara and her fiancé Cusins, a Professor of Greek. Andrew observes the work of a Salvation Army shelter and his daughter's handling of the bully, Bill Walker. When the whole family visits the Undershaft factory and model workers' town, the young idealists are converted to the acceptance of money and power as chief weapons in the fight against evil.

Thanks for the Barbara stuff. If anything else occurs to you, send it along.

I want to get Cusins beyond the point of wanting power. I shall use your passage to bring out the point that Undershaft is a fly on the wheel; but Cusins would not make the mistake of imagining that he could be anything else. The fascination that draws him is the fascination of reality. ... His choice lies between standing on the footplate at work, and merely sitting in a first class carriage reading Ruskin. ... As to the triumph of Undershaft, that is inevitable because I am in the mind that Undershaft is in the right, and that Barbara and Adolphus, with a great deal of his natural insight and cleverness, are very young, very romantic, very academic, very ignorant of the world. I think it would be unnatural if they were able to cope with him. ... Cusins's ... strength lies in the fact that he, like Barbara, refuses the impossibilist position. ...

Shaw, to Professor Gilbert Murray, 7 Oct. 1905, in Gilbert Murray, *An Unfinished Autobiography*, Allen and Unwin, 1960, p. 155-7

'Nonsense! of course it's funny' might be a little peremptory. There are one or two points ... in which Barbara, with all her sweetness, shows that she is her mother's daughter, and that it comes very natural to her to order people about. There is a curious touch of aristocratic pride at the very end, where she says she does not want to die in God's debt, and will forgive him 'as becomes a woman of her rank'. ... Barbara has great courage, great pride, and a high temper at the back of her religious genius; and you need not hesitate to let them flash through at moments if any of the passages catch you that way.

Shaw, to Annie Russell, 20 Nov. 1905, quoted by Bernard Dukore, in *Bernard Shaw, Director*, p. 87

There are no human beings in *Major Barbara*: there are only animated points of view. ... The inter-texture of opinions thus produced is not, of course, a drama, and still less a consistent philosophy. But it is extremely amusing to watch Mr. Shaw busily plying his loom, and bodying forth, thread by thread, the criss-cross pattern of his intellect. ... The play is one long discussion between Barbara, or beneficence through love, and Undershaft, or beneficence through power; and to Undershaft Mr. Shaw resolutely gives the upper hand. He is an admirable figure. There is a passionate and even poetical conviction in many of his sayings that is intensely dramatic and thrilling. But over the Shaw of the past and the Shaw of the present there hovers a third Shaw ... typified in the Euripidean ironist, Adolphus Cusins. He is in love with Barbara and he is hypnotized by Undershaft; but he is not, like them, absorbed in the illusion of the scene; he is at once an actor in their comedy and a dispassionate spectator. His is the philosophical intellect which can get outside of Time and Space, shake off the tyranny of the categories, and criticize the frame of things from the standpoint of pure reason. In short, he is the fundamental, contemplative Shaw. ...

William Archer, *The World*, 5 Dec. 1905

Mr. Shaw has created in *Major Barbara* two characters — Barbara and her father — who live with an intense vitality; a crowd of minor characters that are accurately observed (though some are purposely exaggerated) from life; and one act — the second — which is as cunning and closely knit a piece of craftsmanship as any conventional playwright could achieve, and a cumulative appeal to emotions which no other living playwright has touched. ... During the third act, ... I admit, I found my attention wandering. But this aberration was not due to any loosening of Mr. Shaw's grip on his material. It was due simply to the fact that my emotions had been stirred so much in the previous act that my cerebral machine was not in proper working order. Mr. Shaw ought to have foreseen that effect. In not having done so, he is guilty of a technical error.

Max Beerbohm, *Saturday Review*, 9 Dec. 1905,
reprinted in *Around Theatres*

Charles Laughton and an accomplished troupe have given the play ... a stylish revival ... also a highly stylized one ... illustrative of the character of the work. Essentially what we have here is a dramatic discussion. ... Nothing is permitted to get in the way of this intellectual circus. ... Lady Britomart opens proceedings by walking on stage, closely followed by servants carrying and arranging items of decor. As played by Cornelia Otis Skinner, she is certainly one of the most decorative aspects of this revival, and designer Donald Denslager must have reasoned that his own creations should be spare, streamlined and mobile. ... Altogether ingenious and altogether unobtrusive, as pithy as the play itself. ...

Director Laughton has been just as resourceful. He has staged the production (in two acts) with a casual and sardonic air that Shaw would have admired. ... This is definitely not stylization at the expense of Shaw. ...

Laughton plays Undershaft with every nuance of the diabolical ... and not a trace of Captain Bligh; and Miss Johns brings remarkable emotional range to the girl who sheds her uniform. ...

Theatre Arts, Jan. 1957, p. 97

From a clean, crisp, and inventive production by Clifford Williams the play emerges as a kind of travelling debate, shifting from one location to the next as and where illustrations are needed. It is in many ways a cynical variation on Wilde — *The Importance of Being Undershaft* perhaps; but Shaw's lust for the English language carries it around all the pitfalls of a conversation piece and leads it to an anti-messianic conclusion: what is all human contact but the daily selling of our souls. ... Judi Dench, Elizabeth Spriggs, Brewster Mason, and Richard Pasco are among those who do more than justice to a long-neglected masterpiece.

Sheridan Morley, *Review Copies*, p. 54

The Doctor's Dilemma

'A Tragedy' in four acts and an epilogue.
Written: 1906.
First production: Vedrenne-Barker company, Court Th., 20 Nov. 1906 (dir. Shaw and Granville Barker; with Granville Barker, Lillah McCarthy).
First US production: Wallack's Th., New York, 26 Mar. 1915 (dir. Granville Barker).
Revived: St. James's Th., 6 Dec. 1913 (dir. Granville Barker; with Lillah McCarthy); Everyman Th., Hampstead, 21 Feb. 1921 (dir. Edith Craig; des. Norman Macdermott; with Nicholas Hannen and Felix Aylmer); Everyman Th., 2 Apr. 1923 (dir. and des. Norman Macdermott; with Claud Rains and Cathleen Nesbitt); Kingsway Th., 17 Nov. 1926 (dir. Esmé Percy, who also played Dubedat, with Gwen

Ffrangçon-Davies); Court Th., 13 Jan. 1930 (dir. Esmé Percy; with
Wilfrid Lawson as Sir Patrick); Westminster Th., 17 Feb. 1939
(dir. John Fernald; with Stephen Haggard as Dubedat and Stephen
Murray as Sir Patrick); Whitehall Th., 28 Mar. 1939 (dir. John
Fernald), trans. Whitehall Th., 28 Mar. 1939; Haymarket Th., 4 Mar.
1942 (dir. Irene Hentschel; with Vivien Leigh, and Cyril Cusack, later
John Gielgud and Peter Glenville); Gaiety Th., Dublin, 1947 (with
Cyril Cusack as Dubedat); Birmingham Rep. Th., 6 June 1950
(dir. Douglas Seale); Th. Royal, Brighton, 18 Sept. 1956,
trans. Saville Th., London, 4 Oct. 1956 (dir. Julian Amyes; with Paul
Daneman, Ann Todd, Lewis Casson); Haymarket Th., 23 May 1963
(dir. Donald MacWhinnie; des. Motley; with Brian Bedford and Anna
Massey); Yvonne Arnaud Th., Guildford, 3 May 1966 (dir. Laurier
Lister; des. Hutchinson Scott; with Griffith Jones, Eleanor Bron, and
Max Adrian as B. B.); Chichester Festival Th., 17 May 1972
(dir. John Clements; with Robin Phillips, Joan Plowright, John
Neville); Mermaid Th., 21 Apr. 1975 (dir. Robert Chetwynd; with
Kenneth Cranham, Lynn Farleigh, Nigel Hawthorn, Simon Callow).
First published: in German, 1908; in Hungarian, *c.* 1910.
First published in English: in *The Doctor's Dilemma, Getting Married,
and the Shewing-up of Blanco Posnet,* London: Constable, 1911.
Film: MGM, 1958 (dir. Anthony Asquith; with Dirk Bogarde, Robert
Morley, Felix Aylmer).

---

*The 'tragedy' is a metaphysical concept, not a matter of
emotional perspective. A group of doctors sits in judgement on
the worthiness of the dying Dubedat to be cured, when
resources are scarce. They attempt to weigh his lack of moral
rectitude against his artistic genius. A mistake in treatment
comically hastens the progress of his disease and allows him to
enjoy their discomfiture at his death. The rascal's irreverence
for solemn pretensions focuses a general satire on the medical
profession. The theme of romantic illusion — in Jennifer
Dubedat's love for her husband and in Dr. Ridgeon's infatuation with her — complicates the play.*

You must play Dubedat. Ainley might play him, of course; but he would
look too honest and the enjoyment of the part would set you up for life.
Sir Artegall Osborne is now Sir Ralph Bloomfield-Bonner (familiarly,
B.B.).

        Shaw, to Barker, 28 Aug. 1906, *Shaw-Barker Letters*, p. 70-1

I wish you would suggest a name for yourself in this new play. I cannot very well call the lady Lillah. Provisionally I have called her Andromeda; but Mrs. Andromeda Dubedat is too long. Here in King Arthur's country the name Guinevere survives as Jennifer. ...

Shaw, to Lillah McCarthy, quoted in McCarthy,
Myself and My Friends, Thornton Butterworth, 1933, p. 79-80

Louis Dubedat ... is always scoring. He scores even under the shadow of death. And Mr. Shaw has, moreover, been as anxious to make his death-bed pathetic as was Dickens to make Little Nell's. And, where Dickens failed, Mr. Shaw has succeeded. The pathos here is real. I defy you not to be touched by it, while it lasts. But I defy you, when it is over, to mourn. ...

The posthumous 'one man show' is a revelation of his versatility. Dubedat seems to have caught, in his brief lifetime, the various styles of *all* the young lions of the Carfax Gallery [*which had lent the pictures for the production*] ...

Max Beerbohm, *Saturday Review*, 24 Nov. 1906,
reprinted in *Around Theatres*, second edition, p. 442-4

The last act, in which Dubedat dies in front of the footlights, has been the subject of a good deal of discussion. Mr. Granville Barker acted the death naturally and realistically. Fault was found with him on the ground that a death struggle untouched by artistic emotion is an unfair, unilluminating assault on the emotions. But it was necessary that we should realize that chilly, quiet, matter-of-factness of physical extinction. ... Dubedat hoards his last strength and his last words to stamp an image of himself on his wife's heart which he knows is not the true one. Next to his immortality in his pictures, he values that reincarnation most.

Desmond MacCarthy, *The Court Theatre*

It goes quite splendidly. One is inclined to criticize it in the after-dinner manner of Sir Ralph Bloomfield Bonnington: Delightful evening! Admirable acting! Interesting play! Amusing satire! Charming problem! Stimulating discussion! ... In Dubedat's death scene, Mr. Shaw has managed, by exhibiting death simultaneously from different points of view, to touch an irony he has seldom reached before. ... Mr. Shaw has not put one stroke into drawing [Dubedat's] temperament which reveals force of imagination.

Desmond MacCarthy, *The New Statesman*, 3 Jan. 1914,
reprinted in *Shaw*, p. 73-6

At the Mermaid ... Lynn Farleigh's Jennifer Dubedat was a woman who didn't so much love her ailing husband as regard him as an exciting possession — a relatively unsympathetic reading which in association with Kenneth Cranham's forceful Dubedat, a welcome change from the usual bent elf, made this pair into something more like a partnership of confidence tricksters than a dying artist and his devoted wife. ... It added another dimension to what was in any case an agreeably stimulating evening.

J. W. Lambert, *Drama*, No. 117, Summer 1975, p. 51-2

Getting Married

'A disquisitory play', undivided into acts or scenes.
Written: 1908.
First production: Vedrenne-Barker, Haymarket Th., 12 May 1908
  (dir. Shaw; with Robert Loraine, Henry Ainley, Fanny Brough).
First US production: Booth Th., New York, 6 Nov. 1916 (dir. William
  Faversham).
Revived: Birmingham Repertory Th., 3 Sept. 1921 (dir. A. E. Filmer;
  des. Paul Shelving); Liverpool Playhouse, 1921-22 (dir. Stanley
  Drewitt; des. Doris Zinkiesen); Everyman Th., 27 Mar. 1922
  (dir. Norman Macdermott; with Milton Rosmer, Felix Aylmer,
  Gertrude Kingston); Birmingham Repertory Th., 18 Oct. 1923
  (dir. H. K. Ayliff; des. Paul Shelving); Everyman Th., 9 July 1924
  (dir. Norman Macdermott; with Claude Rains and Edith Evans); Little
  Th., 5 Dec. 1927 (dir. Esmé Percy, who played Hotchkiss); Little Th.,
  25 Nov. 1932 (dir. Milton Rosmer, who played the Bishop, with
  George Hayes and Miriam Lewes); Arts Th., 5 Sept. 1945 (dir. Judith
  Furse; with Alan McClelland, Mark Dignam, Olga Lindo); Arts Th.,
  Cambridge, 15 Nov. 1965 (dir. Eric Jones; des. Kenneth Mellor; with
  Sylvia Coleridge as Mrs. George); Opera House, Manchester, 13 Mar.
  1967, trans. Strand Th., 19 Apr. 1967 (dir. Frank Dunlop; des. Tom
  Lingwood; with Ian Carmichael, Hugh Williams, Alec Clunes,
  Raymond Huntley, Margaret Rawlings, Googie Withers); Malvern
  Festival Th., 1982.
First published: in German, 1910.
First published in English: in *The Doctor's Dilemma, Getting Married,
  and The Shewing-up of Blanco Posnet*, London: Constable, 1911.

The wedding guests gradually assemble in the Bishop's Palace,

*built by the Normans, for the marriage of his daughter, Edith.
She has last-minute doubts and, while she is shut in her room
reading, many different views of marriage, class, and social
organization emerge from the variety of experience and thinking
the assorted characters represent. All are formally dressed, and
the uniforms of various professions emphasize the typical more
than the individual. When the coal-merchant's wife arrives in
mayoral garb, preceded by the Beadle carrying a phallic mace,
the civic and ecclesiastical pageant is complete. Falling into a
prophetic trance, she becomes the voice of irrational power,
dialectically balanced against the ascetic mystical philosophy of
Soames, the Bishop's secretary. The bride and groom having
slipped out in their ordinary clothes to marry privately, the
others process straight to the wedding breakfast.*

If you look at any of the old editions of our classical plays, you will see
that the description of the play is not called a plot or a story, but an
argument. That exactly describes the material of my play. It is an
argument — an argument lasting nearly three hours, and carried on with
unflagging cerebration by twelve people and a beadle.

Shaw, 'Mr. Bernard Shaw on His New Play',
interview drafted for *The Daily Telegraph*, 7 May 1908

I intended long ago writing to tell you how much I enjoyed *Getting
Married*. I like the broad, almost Aristophanic mood and plan, the
entrances of the Goddesses at the end (perhaps too late in the play) and
the prologue spoken by the Greengrocer. ... You will probably hate me,
but I did not think Loraine's part [*Hotchkiss*] quite came off.

Charles Ricketts, letter to Shaw, 12 Aug. 1908, in Ricketts,
Self Portrait, Peter Davies, 1939

The play is all talk; but it is brilliant talk; and however serious in
intention the dialogue is rampageously gay. ... Mr. Shaw's gift for
making people speak out of themselves and lending them, for that
purpose, his own smiting directness of speech tells magnificently. We
are kept alert and amused. ... These discussion plays are thought to be
'formless', and the skill with which Mr. Shaw constructs them has
escaped notice. ... In Hotchkiss we see once more, as in so many scenes
in Mr. Shaw's plays, passion represented in terms of extravagant

59

farce. ... The infatuation of the man is represented as heightened by the dominating violence of the woman. ... These scenes between Hotchkiss and Mrs. George seem to me deplorable; too funny to be serious, and too serious to be funny.

> Desmond MacCarthy, *New Statesman and Nation*, 8 Apr. 1922;
> reprinted in *Shaw*, MacGibbon and Kee, 1951, p. 155-9

The Everyman writes to me about playing Mrs. George 'straight' or otherwise. I always want her to be made up like the Queen [Mary], who is obviously the original and only Mrs. George; but in your case she should be played straight. Fanny Brough, for whom the part was planned, was much older, and had a tragically wrecked face; but you happily have neither of these qualifications. ... Play it your own way; and it will come out a regular dazzler, much more brilliant and fascinating than Millamant.

> Shaw, to Edith Evans, quoted in Bryan Forbes,
> *Ned's Girl*, Elm Tree Books, 1977, p. 84

The Shewing-Up of Blanco Posnet

'A Sermon in Crude Melodrama' in one act.

Written: 1909, for charity performance by Sir Herbert Beerbohm Tree, but banned by Lord Chamberlain.

First production: Abbey Th., Dublin, 25 Aug. 1909 (dir. Sara Allgood and Lady Gregory; with Fred O'Donovan, Arthur Sinclair, Sara Allgood, Maire O'Neill).

First English production: Abbey Players, under auspices of Stage Society, Aldwych Th., 5 and 6 Dec. 1909.

First English public production: Irish Players (Abbey Th. Co.) at Playhouse, Liverpool, 10 Apr. 1916.

Revived: Everyman Th., 14 Mar. 1921 (dir. Edith Craig; des. Norman Macdermott), trans. Queen's Th., 20 July 1921; Shepherd's Bush Th., 29 Nov. 1923 (dir. Andrew Melville); Coliseum Th., 18 Oct. 1926 (dir. Martin Harvey, who played Blanco); Liverpool Playhouse, 1929–30 (dir. William Armstrong); Playhouse Th., London, 12 Feb. 1939 (dir. Esmé Percy, who played Blanco, with Margaret Rawlings, Catherine Lacey); Arts. Th., 16 May 1951 (dir. Stephen Murray; with John Slater, Maurice Denham, Brenda Bruce, Vivienne Bennett); Mermaid Th., 3 Oct. 1961 (dir. Frank Dunlop; with Ronald Fraser and Jill Bennett).

First published: in German, 1910.

First published in English: in *The Doctor's Dilemma, Getting Married, and The Shewing-Up of Blanco Posnet*, London: Constable, 1911.

A drunken horse-thief has, most uncharacteristically, given over a stolen horse for the use of a desperate mother with a sick child. Because of this, he is captured, and put on trial, though the failure of the mother and one other witness to identify him secures his acquittal — to spread the frenzied religiosity with which his good deed has inspired him.

It reproduces in some measure the subject and the feeling of Bret Harte's *Luck of Roaring Camp.* ... The situation — this sketch of a sudden, ruthless, unintelligible interference with the lives of men — though apparently unknown to the Censor, will be familiar to readers of the Bible and of religious poetry and prose, and Mr. Shaw's treatment of it could only offend either the non-religious mind or the sincerely, but conventionally, pious man ... so wrapped up in the emotional view of religion that its sterner and deeper moralities escape him.

The Nation, Sept. 1909

The action unfolds in a wild and woolly city of the Far West, the protagonist is a horse-thief, and the play limits itself to his trial. ...

Posnet ... sets forth some primitive theology. The moment of sentimental weakness in which he yielded to the prayers of a poor mother has been the crisis of his life. The finger of God has touched his brain. ...

The play ends happily. The baby which Posnet tried to save dies, and the mother is apprehended. She tells her story to the court and Posnet is acquitted.

James Joyce, *Il Piccolo della Sera*, Trieste, 5 Sept. 1909,
reprinted in *The Critical Writings of James Joyce*,
ed. E. Mason and R. Ellman, 1939

Misalliance

'A debate in one sitting'.
Written: 1909-10.

First production: Charles Frohman's repertory season, Duke of York's
   Th., 23 Feb. 1910 (dir. Shaw; with Lena Ashwell).
First US production: Broadhurst Th., New York, 27 Sept. 1917
   (prod. William Faversham).
Revived: Everyman Th., Hampstead, 18 Apr. 1922 (dir. Milton Rosmer;
   des. Norman Macdermott; with Dorothy Homes-Gore, Frank Vosper,
   Isabel Jeans); Birmingham Repertory Th., 6 Nov. 1922 (dir. A. E.
   Filmer); Everyman Th., 27 Oct. 1924 (dir. and des. Norman
   Macdermott; with Dorothy Green, Frank Vosper, Leah Bateman, and
   Claude Rains as Percival); Court Th., 17 Mar. 1930 (dir. Esmé Percy,
   who played Julius Baker, with Irene Vanbrugh and Wilfrid Lawson as
   Tarleton); Torch Th., 20 June 1939 (dir. A. E. Filmer; with Dorothy
   Black); 'Q' Th., 16 Jan. 1940 (dir. Godfrey Kenton; with Vivienne
   Bennett, Wilfred Walter as Tarleton, Clifford Evans, Stephen
   Haggard), trans. Embassy Th., 22 Jan. 1940; Arts Th., 10 Aug. 1943
   (dir. Alec Clunes; des. Maise Meiklejohn; with Magda Kun, Peter
   Jones as Julius Baker); Th. Royal, Brighton, 3 Jan. 1956, trans. Lyric
   Th., Hammersmith, 8 Feb. 1956 (dir. Lionel Harris; des. Hutchinson
   Scott; with Miriam Karlin, Roger Livesey, Donald Pleasence, Peter
   Barkworth, Ursula Jeans); Pitlochry Festival Th., 26 May 1956
   (dir. G. Maxwell Jackson); Oxford Playhouse, 9 Oct. 1962 (dir. Frank
   Hauser; des. Desmond Heeley; with Barbara Jefford), trans. Royal
   Court Th., London, 8 Jan. 1963, then Criterion Th., 29 Jan. 1963;
   Mermaid Th., 18 Apr. 1973 (dir. Alan Strachan; des. Bernard
   Culshaw; with Caroline Blakiston and Bill Fraser); Malvern
   Festival Th., 1977; RSC at Barbican, 8 Oct. 1986 (dir. John Caird;
   des. Roger Butlin; with Brian Cox as Tarleton, Jane Lapotaire as
   Lina).
First published: in German, 1910.
First published in English: in *Misalliance, The Dark Lady of the
   Sonnets, and Fanny's First Play*, London: Constable, 1914.

---

*The weekend at the country house of a self-made linen draper,
Tarleton, is fantastically disturbed — by the crash of an aeroplane into the greenhouse, the impact of the pilot and his Polish
superwoman passenger on the household, and the emergence of
an avenging clerk with a gun from a portable Turkish bath.
Order is restored: the pilot stays to marry Tarleton's daughter
Hypatia, while Lina Szczepanowska prepares to soar out of
stuffy domesticity into clearer air, taking the discarded fiancé
with her.*

The debating society of a lunatic asylum — without a motion and without a chairman. That is one surface impression. ... But the second thought is this — it is madness, after all.

The Times, 23 Feb. 1910

Not one [critic] asked why it should not be admirable and enjoyable to push out the dramatic art in new directions. ... *Misalliance* was as enjoyable as was the discomfort of the critics in face of it. ... Mr. Shaw has claimed for it that it is a singularly perfect specimen of high comedy. That is only his fun. There is nothing high about it except its spirits, and they are splendid. ... Shall we call *Misalliance* a symbolist farce?

P. P. Howe, *The Repertory Theatre*, Martin Secker, 1910, p. 92, 101

Plays of discussion that lead nowhere in particular are likely to disappoint their first audiences who naturally expect to be carried to some unusual destination. With the lapse of time, inconclusiveness comes to seem a positive merit.

The Times, 21 June 1939

With its relevance to Women's Lib ... and its gentle mockery of revolution, ... there is no doubt that the revival is what is known as timely — but then almost all of Shaw's plays are at almost all times timely. Beyond that ... the play offers some splendid parts. ... As a plot it does however leave something to be desired: a first half in which nothing happens at all is followed by a second half in which an aeroplane ... crashes through the greenhouse roof and a potential murderer is discovered hiding in a Turkish bath. Strachan's stately production can't do much to help the first, but it does make the most of the second, and Bill Fraser's Tarleton, trapped by his success in underwear, is a constant joy ...

Sheridan Morley, on Mermaid Th. production, June 1973,
reprinted in *Review Copies*, p. 182-3

If *Misalliance* is worth reviving today, it is not for its ideas but for totally other reasons. One is for the Mozartian music of Shaw's prose which just about carries you through the lengthy opening chat. ...

The other is for Shaw's pioneering comic sense which introduces us to Theatre of the Absurd two years before Ionesco was born. Paradoxically, the play takes wing at the very moment when an aeroplane crashes into a Surrey greenhouse and out of it emerges a stunning Polish acrobat (played with implacable feminine fervour by Jane Lapotaire);

and it gathers ever greater momentum with the emergence from a portable Turkish bath of a revolutionary clerk. ...

If there is a governing intention behind John Caird's production it is, I suspect, to anticipate *Heartbreak House* and to suggest that we are watching the terminal decline of Edwardian England. But, theatrically, that matters far less than Shaw's ... bursts of vitality. ... Brian Cox as Tarleton ... beautifully suggests the joy of life surging beneath the mouldering craggy facade of an aged businessman. He looks like an antique ruin inside which there is a crystal fountain ...

Michael Billington, *The Guardian*, 10 October 1986

The Dark Lady of the Sonnets

An interlude.

Written: 1910.

First presented: charity matinee in aid of project for a Shakespeare Memorial National Theatre, Haymarket Th., 24 Nov. 1910 (dir. Shaw and Granville Barker, who also played Shakespeare; des. Charles Ricketts; with Mona Limerick).

First US production: Little Th., Duluth, Minn., 17 Nov. 1914.

First New York production: American National Theatre and Academy, Ziegfeld Th., New York, 29 Jan. 1930.

Revived: Everyman Th., 14 Mar. 1921 (dir. Edith Craig; des. Norman Macdermott; with Nicholas Hannen), trans. Queen's Th., 20 July 1925; Kingsway Th., 17 Sept. 1923 (dir. Harcourt Williams, who played Shakespeare; des. Peggy Fremantle), trans. Coliseum, 29 Oct. 1923; Lyric Th., Hammersmith, 20 Mar. 1926 (dir. Hector Abbas; des. Arthur Phillips; with Milton Rosmer); Old Vic Th., 24 Feb. 1930 (dir. Harcourt Williams, who played Shakespeare; des. Owen P. Smyth; with Martita Hunt and Adèle Dixon); Torch Th., 10 Jan. 1939 (dir. Rupert Scott; with Francis James, Ellen Pollock, Elspeth March); Lyric Th., Hammersmith, 28 Nov. 1944 (dir. Michael Golden; des. Riette Sturge Moore); St. Martin's Th., 3 Apr. 1951 (dir. Ellen Pollock, who played Queen Elizabeth; with Griffith Jones); Arts Th., 27 June 1951 (dir. Roy Rich; des. Ronald Brown; with Maurice Denham, Vivienne Bennett, Rachel Gurney); Pitlochry Festival Th., 7 May 1960 (dir. James Roose Evans); Open Air Th., Regent's Park, 17 July 1978 (dir. Richard Digby Day).

First published: in German, 1910; in English, in *The English Review*, 1911, then in *Misalliance, The Dark Lady of the Sonnets, and Fanny's First Play*, London: Constable, 1914.

Will Shakespeare, waiting for his Dark Lady, encounters a cloaked figure. Revealed to be Queen Elizabeth I, she gives the playwright his opportunity to plead for a National Theatre.

There is again a night background to four figures. Done in the routine way it will be damnable. A few rags and a limelight might work wonders in the right hands.

Shaw, to Charles Ricketts, 1 Nov. 1910

I want these character dresses to move in front of an intense and abnormal starlit sky of a fabulous blue. ... I should like the entrance of Elizabeth to be made in a sudden oblique ray of soft light and to be accompanied by a rush from the wood instruments. I want Barker ... to appear *at first* wrapped in a large grey cloak half statue and half Guy Fawkes. ... The court people ... should wear black and red masks, like Elizabethan maskers, and wear yellow and black dominoes.

Charles Ricketts, to Shaw, Nov. 1910

Fanny's First Play

'An easy play for a little theatre', in three acts, induction and epilogue.
Written: 1911 (new prologue, for Macdona Players, written 1916, but apparently never performed).
First production: Little Th., 19 Apr. 1911 (dir. Shaw, anonymously; with Harcourt Williams, Nigel Playfair, Lillah McCarthy).
First US production: Comedy Th., New York, 16 Sept. 1912 (prod. Sam and Lee Shubert).
Revived: Kingsway Th., 13 Feb. 1915 (dir. Shaw; with Miles Malleson, Lena Ashwell, Henry Ainley, and Ivy St. Helier); Theatre Royal, Birmingham, 18 Sept. 1916 (dir. Charles Macdona); Everyman Th., 6 Feb. 1922 (dir. and des. Norman Macdermott; with Isabel Jeans, Dorothy Holmes-Gore, Milton Rosmer); Everyman Th., 9 July 1923 (dir. George Cass; with Isabel Jeans, Dorothy Massingham, Allan Jeayes); Abbey Th., Dublin, 21 Apr. 1925; Court Th., 4 Mar. 1931 (dir. Charles Macdona; with Iris Baker); Arts Th., 14 Sept. 1944 (dir. Molly Terraine; des. Maise Meiklejohn; with Daphne Arthur); Lyceum Th., Edinburgh, 3 Sept. 1956 (dir. Douglas Seale; with Brenda Bruce, Robin Bailey, Michael Denison); Mermaid Th., 29 Sept. 1965 (dir. Don Taylor; des. Adrian Vaux; with Robert Eddison, Denise Coffey, Timothy Bateson).

First published: in German, 1911;.in English, in *Misalliance, The Dark Lady of the Sonnets, and Fanny's First Play,* London: Constable, 1914.

The play consists of an inset action within a framing dramatic prologue and epilogue (which supported the anonymity of the piece on its first production). A young girl is indulged by her father, a wealthy Irish Count of aesthetic tastes, with the staging of a private performance to which the chief London critics are invited. This is the medium for good-natured satire of some well-known personalities, lightly disguised. The inset realistic comedy is Fanny's rebellious response to her father's attitudes. It depicts a rebellion of children against parents, and of vital instincts against middle-class respectability, which releases the elders in their turn. The engagement of the young couple, Bobby and Margaret, who have both been in prison for being drunk and disorderly, is broken off, and the way is cleared for temperamentally more suitable, but socially disruptive alliances: with a 'daughter of joy' and a butler who is also brother to a duke. Like a signature, Shaw introduces the paradox of the Frenchman who admires outrageous behaviour as typically English. He also sounds deeper and more philosophical notes through Margaret and her mother. Yet, in general, the adoption of a fresh 'young' style and deliberately imitative structure is sustained.

Fanny's First Play was the first of Shaw's to have a long run. ... I cannot understand why he called it 'a pot-boiler'; it belongs to that serious section of his dramatic works, his religious farces. ... And it follows that Mrs. Knox is the linchpin of it. Failure to recognize that was the gravest defect ... of the performance at the Arts Theatre. ...

I missed the prologue and epilogue in which Shaw ridiculed successfully contemporary dramatic critics who run down his plays. I supose they were thought to date too much to interest an audience today. I think the management was wrong ...

Desmond MacCarthy (1940), Shaw, p. 203-5

Androcles and the Lion

'A Fable Play' in two acts, with a prologue.
Written: 1912.
First production: in German, Kleines Th., Berlin, 25 Nov. 1912
(prod. Max Reinhardt), then in Hamburg, July 1913.
First English production: St. James's Th., 1 Sept. 1913 (dir. Granville
Barker; des. Albert Rutherston; with Lillah McCarthy).
First US production: Wallack's Th., New York, 27 Jan. 1915
(dir. Granville Barker; with Lillah McCarthy).
Revived: Abbey Th., Dublin, 4 Nov. 1919; Old Vic Th., 24 Feb. 1930
(dir. Harcourt Williams; with Martita Hunt, Brember Wills, and John
Gielgud as the Emperor); Open Air Th., Regent's Park, 17 July 1937
(dir. Robert Atkins; with Margaretta Scott, Andrew Leigh, and Nigel
Playfair as the Emperor); Winter Garden Th., 20 Sept. 1934
(dir. Robert Atkins; with Margaretta Scott, Andrew Leigh, and Oscar
Asche as the Emperor); Arts Th., 2 Feb. 1943 (dir. Alec Clunes;
des. Rolf Gerard; with Patricia Laffan, and Denys Blakelock as
Androcles); Toynbee Hall, 18 Oct. 1948 (dir. John Allen; with
Vivienne Bennett); Gaiety Th., Dublin, July 1956 (with Cyril
Cusack); Unity Th., 28 Oct. 1960 (dir. Thomas Mercer; des. Nicholas
Ferguson); Mermaid Th., 3 Oct. 1961 (dir. Frank Dunlop; with Jill
Bennett, Edward de Souza); Malvern Festival Th., 29 Aug. 1966
(dir. Bernard Hepton; des. Maurice Strike).
Film: RKO Pictures, 1952 (prod. Gabriel Pascal; dir. Chester Erskine;
with Jean Simmons, Victor Mature as the Captain, Maurice Evans as
the Emperor, and Robert Newton as Ferrovius).
First published: in German, 1913; in English in USA, 1914.
First published in England: in *Androcles and the Lion, Overruled,
Pygmalion*, London: Constable, 1916.

---

*In the prologue, the timid Christian tailor, Androcles, burdened
with a nagging wife, removes a thorn from a lion's paw. This
introduces the themes of courage and strength involved in
the main action, concerning a group of Christian prisoners,
Androcles among them, destined for the lions in the Coliseum at
the Emperor's pleasure. The nature of faith and the strength of
spiritual integrity are matters explored in argument between the
lovely Lavinia and the young captain who wants her to save
herself by recanting: Ferrovius discovers that he has to be
true to the physical power with which he is endowed, while*

Androcles and his lion meet in friendship in the arena, and their joyful encounter causes the Emperor's conversion to Christianity.

[Shaw] invented a new form, the religious pantomime. *Androcles and the Lion* is the reverse of medieval in sentiment and doctrine, but its nearest parallel as a dramatic entertainment is one of those old miracle plays in which buffoonery and religion were mixed pell-mell together. ...

An English audience has not as a rule sufficient emotional mobility to follow a method which alternates laughter with pathos, philosophy with fun, in such rapid succession.

Desmond McCarthy, *New Statesman*, 6 Sept. 1913,
reprinted in *Shaw*, p. 102

I once got carried away by a current in a rough sea; and ... I was absolutely certain that I was on the point of inevitable death. The effect was to destroy the whole interest and importance of my imaginary world, usually the largest part of my world. ... This is what leads me to believe that the effect of martyrdom — or rather of waiting for martyrdom — would be to test one's religion very severely by destroying all the imaginary and romantic part of it. ... Thus the martyr is the person whose faith survives the wreck of his (or her) beliefs. Spintho, the gentleman who walked into the lion's mouth, had all the beliefs, but no faith, and collapsed when the beliefs were put out of countenance by death.

Shaw, to Rosina Filippi, 16 Sept. 1913, *Collected Letters*, 3, p. 203-4

Pygmalion

A 'Romance' in five acts.
Written: 1912-13.
First production: in German, Hofburg Th., Vienna, 16 Oct. 1913
(dir. Hugo Thimig; with Max Paulsen and Lilli Marberg).
First English production: His Majesty's Th., 11 Apr. 1914 (dir. Shaw;
des. A. E. Craven and Denis Mackail; with Herbert Beerbohm Tree
and Mrs. Patrick Campbell).
Revived: Aldwych Th., 10 Feb. 1920 (dir. Shaw; des. Denis Mackail;
with C. Aubrey Smith and Mrs. Patrick Campbell), trans. Duke of
York's Th., 10 May 1920 (with cast changes); Kingsway Th.,

19 Jan. 1927 (dir. Esmé Percy, who played Higgins, with Gwen
Ffrangçon-Davies); Court Th., 30 Dec. 1929 (dir. Esmé Percy, who
played Higgins, with Margaret Macdona and Wilfrid Lawson);
Court Th., 13 Apr. 1931 (dir. Esmé Percy, who played Higgins, with
Margaret Macdona and George Merritt); Cambridge Th., 3 Sept. 1935
(dir. Esmé Percy, who played Higgins, with Margaret Rawlings); Old
Vic Th., 21 Sept. 1937 (dir. Tyrone Guthrie; des. Molly McArthur;
with Robert Morley, Diana Wynyard); Embassy Th., 29 May 1939
(dir. Campbell Gullan; des. Leon Davey; with Basil Sydney, Lewis
Casson, Margaret Rawlings), trans. 'Q' Th., 5 June 1939, trans.
Haymarket Th., 13 June 1939; Lyric Th., Hammersmith (dir. Ellen
Pollock and Michael Golden, who played the lead roles); Lyric Th.,
Hammersmith, 18 June 1947 (dir. Peter Ashmore; des. Kathleen
Ankers; with Alec Clunes, Brenda Bruce, Mervyn Johns);
Bedford Th., Camden Town, 23 May 1949 (dir. Douglas Seale);
Embassy Th., 23 Jan. 1951 (dir. Michael Langham; des. John
Pemberton; with Robin Bailey, Yvonne Mitchell, and Gordon Harker
as Doolittle); Th. Royal, Nottingham, 14 Aug. 1951 (dir. Peter Potter;
with Margaret Lockwood, Alan Webb), trans. Lyceum Th.,
Edinburgh, 19 Aug. 1951; Royal Court Th., Liverpool, 20 Oct. 1953,
trans. St. James's Th., 19 Nov. 1953 (dir. John Clements, who played
Higgins; des. Laurence Irving and Elizabeth Haffenden; with Kay
Hammond, Nicholas Hannen, Athene Seyler); Th. Royal, Bristol,
12 Mar. 1957 (dir. John Harrison; des. Rosemary Vercoe; with Joseph
O'Conor, Wendy Williams, and Peter O'Toole as Doolittle);
Pembroke Th., Croydon, 29 Mar. 1960 (dir. Ellen Pollock; with Sarah
Churchill, Michael Golden); Pitlochry Festival Th., 21 Apr. 1962
(dir. William Moore); Albery Th., 15 May 1974 (dir. John Dexter;
des. Jocelyn Herbert and Andrew Sanders; with Diana Rigg, Alec
McCowen, Bob Hoskins); Belgrade Th., Coventry, 1975; Malvern
Festival Th., Aug. 1978 (with Paul Daneman); Shaftesbury Th.,
10 May 1984 (dir. Ray Cooney; des. Douglas Heap; with Peter
O'Toole), revived Plymouth Th., New York, 1987 (with Sir John
Mills as Doolittle).
Films: in German, 1935 (dir. Erich Engel; with Gustaf Gründgens,
Jenny Jugo); in Dutch, 1937 (dir. Ludwig Berger; with Lily
Bouwmeester, Johan de Meester); in English, 1938 (dir. Gabriel
Pascal; with Wendy Hiller, Leslie Howard, Wilfrid Lawson). Screen
version *published:* London: Constable (Standard Edition), 1941.
Musical adaptation: as *My Fair Lady*, 1955 (book by Alan J. Lerner;
music by Frederick Loewe), *published:* Penguin Books, 1958.
First published: in German, 1913; in Hungarian, 1914; in Swedish,
1914.
First US edition: serialized in *Everybody's Magazine*, New York, 1914.

First English edition: in *Androcles and the Lion, Overruled, Pygmalion,* London: Constable, 1916.

Philologist Henry Higgins lays a bet that by taking her pronunciation in hand, he will pass off a cockney guttersnipe as a lady in six months. Correct speech and fine clothes turn Eliza into an automaton, and more is involved before the bet is won. The final stage comes when the man-made lady rebels against her creator. In a secondary plot, Eliza's dustman father, Alfred Doolittle, is transformed into a wealthy man and finds that his change of social class inhibits his vitality.

I must have my Liza and no other Liza. There is no other Liza and can be no other Liza. I wrote the play to have my Liza.

Shaw, to Mrs. Patrick Campbell, 5 July 1912, *Collected Letters,* 3, p. 97

I wrote a play for Alexander which was really a play for Mrs. Patrick Campbell. It is almost as wonderful a fit as Brassbound [for Henry Irving and Ellen Terry]; for I am a good ladies' tailor, whatever my shortcomings may be.

Shaw, to Ellen Terry, 20 Aug. 1912, *Collected Letters,* 3, p. 110

It is my intention to produce *Pygmalion* here anonymously. The part of Eliza is to be played by Mrs. Patrick Campbell; and the play will be announced as 'By a Fellow of the Royal Society of Literature'. This will give the idea that it is a classical play, and that Mrs. Campbell is to appear as Galatea. As she has never appeared in a low-life part, the surprise will be complete. [*This plan was abandoned when the play received its first performance, in Trebitsch's translation, in Vienna.*]

Shaw, to Siegfried Trebitsch, 29 Jan. 1913, *Collected Letters,* 3, p. 146-7

I give up in despair that note of terror in the first scene which collects the crowds and suddenly shows the audience that there is a play there, and a human soul there, and a social problem there, and a formidable capacity for feeling in the trivial giggles of the comic passages. But until you get it I shall never admit that you can play Eliza, or play Shaw.

The danger tonight will be a collapse of the play after the third act. I am sending a letter to Tree which will pull him together if it does not kill him. ... I have forced half the battle on you; but winning half the battle will not avert defeat. ... You think you like fighting; and now you will have to succeed sword in hand. You have left yourself poorly provided with ideas and expedients; and you must make up for them by dash and brilliancy and resolution.

> Shaw, to Mrs. Patrick Campbell, 11 Apr. 1914,
> *Collected Letters*, 3, p. 224

The tragedy comes in the fate of the flower girl's father, whose story is really a modern version of the old Don Juan play, *Il Dissoluto Punito*. This man is an Immoralist, a lover of wine, women, and song, a flouter of respectability, one whose delight it is to *épater le bourgeois*.

In the old play he is cast into Hell by the statue of the man he has murdered. In my play a far more real and terrible fate overtakes him. ... Something quite simple, quite respectable, quite presentable to the youngest schoolgirl. And yet a fearful retribution.

> Shaw, fragment for an interview, in *Collected Plays*, IV, p. 800

Mr. Higgins's task was merely to transmute one kind of slang into another. ... As for the girl herself, all that was necessary was to devitalize and disembody her — to turn something into nothing. These tasks Mr. Higgins duly accomplished. ... When she asks him for a share in life, ... Higgins, artificer in flesh and blood, has done with her. So the girl turns on her brutal trainer, and shows him the kind of man he is. ... Now, this is assuredly a good subject, well suited to Mr. Shaw's fashion of holding romance upside down. ... What I complain of is that with his reserves and ironies, and by a certain caprice and waywardness of thought, Mr. Shaw has failed to show his audience precisely what he meant.

> H. W. Massingham, *The Nation*, 18 Apr. 1914

I hardly know how to tackle a play which bristles with so many points, especially as I must confess that I am not certain I understood the play as a whole. Has it an idea or does it simply bristle? ... Perhaps when I read my fellow critics I shall discover that what I found with effort was quite obvious to them. In that case I retract in advance the criticism that Mr. Shaw has huddled up his climax, and failed to arrange the perspective of the dialogue so that the mind is led easily up to the central point. Now the last act is, and is not, a love scene; Pygmalion–Higgins, like other Shavian heroes, is running away from passion ... but when [Eliza] runs away he is frantic to get her back. The question is on what terms. ... Then she turns on him ... shakes him off and stands on her own feet as an independent human being. ... Henceforth she is a person he can reckon upon, and his fear of her disappears. That I take it is the theme of the play.

Higgins is called a professor of phonetics, but he is really an artist — that is the interesting thing about him, and his character is a study of the creative temperament. ...

> Desmond McCarthy, *The New Statesman*, 18 Apr. 1914,
> reprinted in *Shaw*, Macgibbon and Kee, 1951, p. 108-10

The part of Eliza was written for Mrs. Campbell. There are passages in it which could only have been written by a dramatist who delighted in the temperament of that great actress as well as in her art. ... No doubt colour has faded from what was the brightest dab of it in her part. ... True, 'bloody' still gets its laugh, but it no longer releases the roar that greets the crash of a taboo.

> Desmond MacCarthy, on the film version,
> *New Statesman and Nation*, 1 July 1939, reprinted in *Drama*, p. 112

Let us forget about the hysteria associated with *My Fair Lady* and point instead to the rare, serene pleasure it communicates, ... arising from the fact that it treats both the audience and *Pygmalion* with civilized respect. ... Everything in the score grows naturally out of the text and the characters; the authors have trusted Shaw, and we, accordingly, trust them. Consider the four solo numbers they have provided for Higgins. ... All four songs are right in character, and all four are written more to be acted than sung. ... For all its grace and buoyancy, what holds the show together at the last is its determination to put character first.

> Kenneth Tynan, *Curtains*, p. 281-2

Here was something we hadn't seen for years. ... Professor Higgins was not Rex Harrison. ... Instead, he was Alec McCowen and something much nearer your hard-line male chauvinist. ... John Dexter ... has clapped a repossession order on a play presumed lost to Julie Andrews and Cecil Beaton, and shown us that the quintessence of Ibsenism, as mediated by Shaw, still has power to hurt in 1974. ...

One no more expects [Diana Rigg as Eliza] to remain on speaking terms with the cruel tyrant, Higgins, than Nora to return to the marital dovecote after the end of *A Doll's House*. ... Stepney with Sylvia Pankhurst, or Holloway with Emmeline, would be more congenial, considering she has (and *knows* she has) been contemptuously severed from her roots, ... patronized as a woman, held captive to satisfy a man's gambling instinct, and educated to be a lady, that is to say an inanimate piece of drawing room decoration without apparent purpose or function.

Benedict Nightingale, *New Statesman*, 24 May 1974

O'Flaherty, V.C.

'A recruiting pamphlet' in one act.
Written: 1915.
First (amateur) production: with officers of the Fortieth Squadron, Royal Flying Corps, on the Western Front, Treizennes, Belgium, 17 Feb. 1917 (dir. Robert Loraine, who played the title role).
First US production: 39th Street Th., New York, 21 June 1920 (Deborah Bierne Irish Players, with P. J. Kelly in the lead).
First English production: Stage Society, Lyric Th., Hammersmith, 19 and 20 Dec. 1920 (dir. Shaw; with Arthur Sinclair and Sara Allgood).
Revived: Arts Th., 27 June 1951 (dir. Roy Rich; with Alan MacNaughtan, Brenda Bruce); Mermaid Th., 14 Sept. 1966 (dir. Peter Gill; with Ian McKellen, Marie Kean); Gaiety Th., Dublin, 3 Oct. 1967 (dir. Sean Cotter; with Donal McCann).
First published: in USA, 1917; in England, in *Heartbreak House, Great Catherine, and Playlets of the War*, London: Constable, 1919.

An Irish private returns home — to the initial disgust of his mother and sweetheart for having fought in the English army. He appeases them with presents and pay, but eventually throws them out, reflecting on the relative 'peace' of the western front.

O'Flaherty, V.C. ... almost persuades one that it is major Shaw. ... Dramatically, its fatal weakness is the tremendous (and protracted) build-up for the mother who, when she appears, is only provided with a few minutes of conventional harangue. ... Ian McKellen is quite brilliant in the title role: a sustained piece of bravura acting.

Frank Marcus, *Plays and Players*, Nov. 1966, p. 15

Heartbreak House

'A Fantasia in the Russian Manner on English Themes' in three acts.
Written: at intervals, 1913-16.
First production: Theatre Guild, Garrick Th., New York, 10 Nov. 1920
(dir. Dudley Digges; des. Lee Simonson).
First English production: Royal Court Th., 18 Oct. 1921 (dir. Shaw and
J. B. Fagan; with Brember Wills, Ellen O'Malley, Mary Greg as
Hesione, Edith Evans as Ariadne).
Revived: Birmingham Repertory Th., 3 Mar. 1923 (dir. H. K. Ayliff;
des. Paul Shelving); Queen's Th., 25 Apr. 1932 (Birmingham
Repertory Company, dir. H. K. Ayliff; des. Paul Shelving; with
Cedric Hardwicke, Edith Evans as Ariadne, Wilfrid Lawson as
Mangan); Westminster Th. 9 Mar. 1937 (dir. Michael MacOwan;
des. Peter Goffin; with Cecil Trouncer, Richard Goolden as Mazzini
Dunn); Cambridge Th., 18 Mar. 1943 (dir. John Burrell; des.
Michael Relph; costumes, Cecil Beaton; with Robert Donat, replaced
during run by John Laurie, Deborah Kerr as Ellie, Edith Evans as
Hesione); Arts Th., 5 July 1950 (dir. John Fernald; des. Ronald
Brown; with Walter Fitzgerald, and Catherine Lacey as Hesione);
Oxford Playhouse, 2 Oct. 1961 (dir. Frank Hauser; des. Pauline
Whitehouse and Philip Prowse; with Roger Livesey, Dulcie Gray,
Judy Campbell, Perlita Neilson, and Michael Denison as Hector),
trans. Wyndham's Th., 1 Nov. 1961; Chichester Festival Th.,
18 July 1967 (dir. John Clements, who also played Shotover), trans.
Lyric Th., London, 9 Nov. 1967; National Theatre at Old Vic Th.,
25 Feb. 1975 (dir. John Schlesinger; des. Michael Annals; with
Colin Blakely, Kate Nelligan, Eileen Atkins, Anna Massey, Paul
Rogers); Nottingham Playhouse, 1979; Malvern Festival Th.,
Aug. 1981 (with Anthony Quayle, Patrick Cargill, Barbara Murray
and Mel Martin); Royal Exchange Th., Manchester, 29 Oct. 1981
(dir. Jonathan Hales; des. Roger Butlin and Deirdre Clancy; with
Alfred Burke, Eleanor Bron, Nigel Stock as Mangan); Haymarket
Th., 10 Mar. 1983 (dir. John Dexter; des. Jocelyn Herbert; with Rex
Harrison and Diana Rigg).
First published: in *Heartbreak House, Great Catherine, and Playlets of
the War*, London: Constable, 1919.

---

*A house like a ship is the setting for a symbolic fantasy, in which
Hermione Hushabye, daughter of ex-sea captain and inventor
Shotover, has invited for the weekend young Ellie Dunne, her
well-intentioned but ineffectual father, Mazzini, and the wealthy*

industrialist, Mangan, who wants to marry Ellie. The romantic hero she loves proves to be Hermione's husband. Uninvited guests arrive: Shotover's other daughter, Lady Utterword, with her follower, Randall, and a burglar who steals her necklace. Ellie hypnotizes Mangan and forms a spiritual alliance with Shotover. An air raid kills Mangan and the burglar — who have hidden in the pit where the Captain keeps his dynamite — but brings regeneration to the others.

The sound of the Zepp's engines was so fine, and its voyage through the stars so enchanting, that I positively caught myself hoping next night that there would be another raid. ... One is so pleased at having seen the show that the destruction of a dozen people or so in hideous terror and torment does not count.

> Shaw, to Sidney and Beatrice Webb, 5 Oct. 1916,
> *Collected Letters*, 3, p. 426

There is a play of mine called *Heartbreak House* which I always connect with you because I conceived it in that house somewhere in Sussex where I first met you and, of course, fell in love with you.

> Shaw, to Virginia Woolf, 10 May 1940, quoted by Leonard Woolf,
> in *Beginning Again*, Hogarth Press, 1964

In Vienna ... the atmosphere of the piece was missed; the sexually attractive parts were given to elderly actresses without charm and the virginal heroine given to the siren of the company. ... There is not a line that will not make its effect if it is properly delivered, and if the atmosphere which makes the play a picture of a house, an enchanted, amazing sort of house, is created. ... [Ellie's] spiritual marriage with the old captain must be like the marriage by which a nun is made the bride of Christ.

> Shaw, to Tor Hedberg (for Karl Hedberg), 27 Sept. 1921,
> *Collected Letters*, 3, p. 734

Ellie is technically the heavy lead in the play.

> Shaw, to Arnold Bennett, 20 Oct. 1921, *Collected Letters*, 3, p. 741

The part of Ellie is written with obvious operatic solos in it; and Ellen

[O'Malley] quite understood that game ... and delivered them accordingly. And immediately the old outcry begins against recitations, against sing-song, against talking as if in a trance ... and all the rest of it. The odd thing is that though Hector declaims all through like him of Troy, and the Captain prophesies like a David, nobody challenges their right to do it. ... I like that sort of thing and write for it when I want it.

Shaw, to St. John Ervine, 23 Oct. 1921, *Collected Letters*, 3, p. 743

You have to get Ibsen thoroughly in mind if you are not to find the Zeppelin at the end of Shaw's play merely monstrous. It has already destroyed the people who achieve; it is to come again to lighten the talkers' darkness, and [to] the peril of all the happy homes in the neighbourhood. ... The characters in this play are nearer to apes and goats than to men and women. Shall they nevertheless persist in being themselves, or shall they pray to be Zeppelin-destroyed and born again? ...

It were easy to find a surface resemblance between *Heartbreak House* and *Crotchet Castle* ... this play of wooden plot and inflated symbol. ... The old man, with his soul divinely loose about him, has something of the moral grandeur of Job, the intelletual stature of Isaiah. There is pathos in him. ...

The play stands or falls exactly as we get or miss this spiritual hang. As an entertainment pure and simple it is dull and incoherent — even for Shaw. ... I found it quite definitely exhilarating and deeply moving, and it therefore ranks for me among the great testaments. When I saw it at the Court Theatre it was admirably acted.

James Agate, *Saturday Review*, 21 Oct. 1921

Mr. Shaw is gloriously an artist in his sense of the importance of ideas, and in his sense of a subject, but he is without artistic respect for unity of effect. ... His high spirits are a wonderful gift, but they master and distract him, and they have seriously damaged this fine play.

Desmond MacCarthy, *New Statesman*, 29 Oct. 1921

It has form as well as substance. ... Its humour and its argument, instead of being to each other as a showman's rattle might be to his oratory, are felt to be necessary and independent parts of the same composition.

The Times

Shaw's interest in people ... is in people *primarily* as social beings. ...

In *Heartbreak House* — which in the order of his works lies at the turning point between the brilliantly complete comedies and the looser disquisitions of the later period — he has not established for them, hardly even indicated, the framework of a social order. ... It is this, I think, which gives the play its curious air of being hung out in Nowhere. And what gives it its air of having more feeling lying about it, is that the prevailing mood is unexpected, and ... unique in Shaw's work. ... Here there is a languor, a diffused sense of disillusion. ...

It is the last act ... which has a real sort of perfection about it. ... Where this play does resemble Chekhov is that each of the characters is vital to the whole design and each must be right; and not all the company seem ... quite up to it. The burden has to be carried too much by the dazzling pointing, timing, and backing up of Miss Catherine Lacey, and the wonderfully telling irruptions of Walter Fitzgerald ...

T. C. Worsley, *The Fugitive Art*, John Lehmann, 1952, p. 150

The mood is as near to nihilism as Shaw ever ventured. ...

Shaw is constitutionally unable to be mystic or melancholy, or even very serious, for long. ... There's no more suffering or evil in this Shavian hothouse than there's Chekhovian mystery.

Benedict Nightingale, *New Statesman*, 7 Mar. 1975

Never mind the plot, which barely exists: feel the passion, which indisputably does. ... Yet the company isn't collectively alert and responsive enough to cohere into ... an ensemble. Or isn't until the very end when ... momentarily, we sense the play's force and gravity; and then it is over.

Benedict Nightingale, *New Statesman*, 18 Mar. 1983

Back to Methuselah

A play cycle in five parts.
Written: 1918-20.
First US production: Theatre Guild, Garrick Th., New York:
   Parts I and II, 27 Feb. 1922; Parts III and IV, 6 Mar. 1922; Part V,
   13 Mar. 1922 (dir. Philip Moeller; des. Lee Simonson).
First English production: Birmingham Repertory Th.: Part I,
   9 Oct. 1923; Part II, 10 Oct. 1923; Part III, 11 Oct. 1923 (matinee);
   Part IV, 11 Oct. 1923 (evening); Part V, 12 Oct. 1923
   (dir. H. K. Ayliff; des. Paul Shelving; with Edith Evans,

Cedric Hardwicke, Gwen Ffrangçon-Davies), trans. Court Th.,
London: Part I, 18 Feb. 1924; Part II, 19 Feb. 1924; Part III,
20 Feb. 1924; Part IV, 21 Feb. 1924; Part V, 22 Feb. 1924 (with
Caroline Keith replacing Edith Evans).

Revived: Malvern Festival Th.: Parts I and II, 20 Aug. 1929; Parts III
and IV, 21 Aug. 1929; Part V, 22 Aug. 1929 (dir. H. K. Ayliff; des.
Paul Shelving; with Edith Evans, Cedric Hardwicke, but many
changes from 1923 cast); Parts I and V, Court Th. 10 and 11 Sept.
1924 (dir. H. K. Ayliff; des. Paul Shelving; with Edith Evans,
Gwen Ffrangçon-Davies, Cedric Hardwicke), Part I only revived,
Court Th., 10 May 1926 (with Caroline Keith replacing Edith Evans);
entire cycle, Court Th., 5-19 Mar. 1928 (dir. H. K. Ayliff;
des. Paul Shelving; with Edith Evans, Gwen Ffrangçon-Davies,
Cedric Hardwicke, Laurence Olivier as Martellus, and Ralph
Richardson as Pygmalion); Part I only, New Lindsey Th.,
27 Aug. 1946 (dir. Peter Cotes; des. Richard Lake); entire cycle,
Arts Th., 18 Feb.-4 Mar. 1947 (dir. Noel Willman; des. Fanny Taylor
and Michael Warre; with Vivienne Bennett and Michael Gwynne);
version abridged by Arnold Moss, tour of 42 North American cities
before 'dying' in New York, 1957 (dir. Margaret Webster; with
Tyrone Power); National Theatre at Old Vic Th., Parts I, II, and III
(as Part I), 31 July 1969; Parts IV and V (as Part II), 1 Aug. 1969
(dir. Clifford Williams and Donald Mackechnie; des. Ralph Koltai;
with Ronald Pickup, Charles Kay, and Joan Plowright as the Voice of
Lilith); Shaw Th., 18-19 June 1984 (dir. Bill Pryde; des. Poppy
Mitchell); entire cycle, Shaw Festival, Niagara-on-the-Lake, 15 Aug.
1986 (dir. Denise Coffey; des. Cameron Porteous).

First published: New York: Brentano's, 1921; London: Constable, 1921.

*A cycle of five plays, of which Part I is an overture, introducing
the main themes. Shaw's version of the Book of Genesis
concentrates, first, on Adam and Eve's choice of reproductive
continuity in place of immortality, with ironic interpolations
from the Serpent; then on Cain's opposition of the death-instinct
to his parents' unsophisticated cultivation of life.*

*Part II is realistic in form, a combination of drawing-room
comedy and contemporary political satire, in which a philosopher and a biologist, the Barnabas brothers, outline to two
visiting politicians (based on Asquith and Lloyd George) their
argument that the term of human life needs to be extended to
300 years, if the government of the modern world, inaugurated*

by the disaster of the First World War, and the solution of its greatest problems are to be humanly feasible.

Part III is a Gilbertian fantasy of Britain in the twenty-first century, with politicians shallower and sillier than ever, and the country being run by permanent officials drawn from formerly subject races. The first of the long-livers emerge — Conrad Barnabas's parlourmaid and the curate from Part II, now in full maturity of mind.

Part IV takes place a thousand years on, near Galway Bay. The division of long-livers from short-livers is complete. The tragic hero of this play is the Elderly Gentleman, who has come from Baghdad in the party of Emperor Napoleon of Turania to consult the Oracle on the best date for a general election. Through successive dialogues, mainly with a long-living 'flapper' (a new version of Savvy Barnabas), the Elderly Gentleman comes to appreciate the values of the long-livers without having the capacity to live as they do. Unable to go on living in either of the worlds he knows, he dies of discouragement.

Part V projects us into a remote Utopia where there are no short-livers, but only Children and Ancients. A human being emerges physically full-grown from an egg; the Youths and Maidens of the chorus attending this ceremony pass within three years through the attitudes and emotions we associate with youth, maturity, and social life, on the way to a virtually eternal state of solitary contemplation. The play completes its circle. The voices of Adam and Eve, Cain, and the Serpent are heard out of the darkness, then give way to the voice of Lilith, the creative spirit or life-force personified.

I ... am worse bored by the Brothers Barnabas than by their unfortunate family and rector. I shall have to get the picture better composed; but I don't think it will come to a Socratic dialogue pure and simple. The idea is not to get comic relief (they are not really comic, if you come to that); but to exhibit the church, marriage, the family, and parliament under shortlived conditions before reproducing them under longlived conditions. ... I may have to disregard the boredom of the spectator who has not mastered all the motifs, as Wagner had to do; but I daresay I shall manage to make the people more amusing, some of them more poetic, and all of them more intelligible than they now are in this first draft.

Shaw, to Granville Barker, 18 Dec. 1918, *Collected Letters*, 3, p. 575

Part III: I hate. You seem to me to be kicking the wretched Asquith-George long after he is spiritually dead. ...

Part IV: I like best of all. ... The ingredients — the satire, the fantasy and the rest — seem to me better mixed. The whole thing balances better dramatically.

Part V: is Gulliver in excelsis. But it raises one question: how far can one use pure satire in the theatre? For satire scarifies humanity. The theatre uses it as a medium and must therefore be tender to it. Now in Part V it is quite possible that the automata would be the most moving and appealing figures. ... Perfect formality may be dramatically (interpretively) speaking what it will need.

> Granville Barker, to Shaw, 9 Feb. 1921, quoted in
> *Granville Barker and His Correspondents*, ed. Eric Salmon,
> Detroit: Wayne University Press, 1986, p. 155-6

Cain should open this scene (Part I, Act II) in a quite modern vein, with the high-pitch and haw-haw of a stage cavalry officer, and with conceited superiority and self-satisfaction. He is not a savage. By contrast with Adam he is a highly civilized gentleman. He does not scowl; his swagger is a gay swagger. He patronizes his parents.

> Shaw, advice to Scott Sunderland, quoted in G. W. Bishop,
> *Barry Jackson and the London Theatre*, p. 28

In the New York production it was Part II, about which Mr. Shaw had expressed a doubt for American audiences, that was the most popular. In Berlin it created such a *furore* that the manager broke his contract and ran it night after night, abandoning the rest of the pentateuch.

> G. W. Bishop, *Barry Jackson and the London Theatre*, p. 31

The last phase of *Back to Methuselah* is the most moving thing that it has been my fortune to see on the stage. ... Mr. Paul Shelving's settings were beyond all praise, for the glade, which had an arcadian peace until it was transformed to the whiteness of eternal snows, was exactly what was needed to give life to Mr. Shaw's dream.

> [R. Crompton Rhodes], *Birmingham Post*, 13 Oct. 1923

Methuselah is a tremendous effort of the imagination on the part of a man who in some directions has obviously deep insight, to express his sense of the meaning of life. It cannot be boring to anyone who even in the interstices of wool-gathering, work, and distractions, has tried to think — unless such a person has thought beyond the dramatist. ... The impression made by these clean, cool, bald, gentle old creatures, with mysterious psychic powers (admirably acted by Miss Edith Evans and Mr. Cedric Hardwicke) is, on the stage, exactly that of Buddhist saints, far advanced in disentangling themselves fromt the wheel of life, but still far from Nirvana.

Desmond MacCarthy, 11 Oct. 1924,
reprinted in *Shaw*, p. 139-40

...Without dramatic life or coherence. ... I could not believe for one minute that the company had the smallest faith in the writing.

Irving Wardle, *The Times*, 4 Aug. 1969

The scene for this 'meta-biological pentateuch' was dazzlingly set by Ralph Koltai in a shimmering perspex limbo of considerable beauty. Electronic bells boomed, a great pulse throbbed, the earth moved round an elipsed sun. ... Only in *The Gospel of the Brothers Barnabas*, good standard Shavian dialectic drama, did the piece hold up. ... A summary dismissal, I fear, for a major undertaking; but at least the National Theatre Company, more than loyal to its author, did with style what it exists to do.

J. W. Lambert, *Drama*, No. 95, Winter 1969, p. 25

Bill Pryde and his accomplished team of nine actors have already scotched the notion that it's an intractable masterpiece. Pryde's decision to set the proceedings in a rehearsal room of the 'twenties, with Shaw himself sitting in offering the actors (and audience) encouragement and explanation, is a brilliant and helpful device.

Malcolm Hay, *Time Out*, 21 June 1984

Inevitably, in a production so bare, with characters like the Serpent, Lilith, Ozymandias, Cleopatra and the Ancients all dressed in twentieth-century clothes, something is forfeited. But the play still emerges as one of the towering achievements of modern theatre.

Francis King, *Sunday Telegraph*, 1 July 1984

Saint Joan

A chronicle play in six scenes and an epilogue.
Written: 1923.
First US production: Theatre Guild, Garrick Th., New York,
  28 Dec. 1923 (dir. Philip Moeller; des. Raymond Dorey; with
  Winifred Lenihan and Maurice Colbourne).
First English production: New Th., 26 Mar. 1924 (dir. Shaw and
  Lewis Casson; des. Charles Ricketts; with Sybil Thorndike and
  Ernest Thesiger).
Revived: Regent Th., 14 Jan. 1925 (dir. Lewis Casson; des. Charles
  Ricketts; with Sybil Thorndike and Ernest Thesiger), revived
  Lyceum Th., 24 Mar. 1926 (with some cast changes, Harold Scott
  replacing Ernest Thesiger); in French, Globe Th., 10 June 1930
  (dir. and des. Georges Pitoëff; with Ludmille Pitoëff); His
  Majesty's Th., 6 Apr. 1931 (dir. Lewis Casson; des. Charles Ricketts;
  with Sybil Thorndike); Old Vic Th., 26 Nov. 1934
  (dir. David Ffolkes; with Mary Newcombe, Maurice Evans,
  Leo Genn, Felix Aylmer, Cecil Trouncer); Streatham Hill Th.,
  10 Oct. 1939 (dir. Esmé Church; des. James Hoyle; with
  Constance Cummings); King's Th., Hammersmith, 19 Feb. 1945
  (dir. Lewis Casson; des. Peter Coffin; with Ann Casson); King's Th.,
  Hammersmith, 7 Mar. 1946 (dir. Lewis Casson; with Ann Casson);
  Old Vic Company at New Th., 3 Dec. 1947 (dir. John Burrell;
  des. Michael Warre and Alix Stone; with Celia Johnson, Alec
  Guinness, Harry Andrews, Bernard Miles); Th. Royal, Bristol (dir.
  Denis Carey; with Pamela Alan, Donald Pleasence, John Neville as
  Dunois); Arts Th., Cambridge, 20 Sept. 1954 (dir. John Fernald;
  des. Paul Mayo and Michael Ellis; with Siobhan McKenna and
  Kenneth Williams), trans. Arts Th., London, 29 Sept. 1954,
  trans. St. Martin's Th., 9 Feb. 1955; Library Th., Manchester, 8 Feb.
  1956 (dir. Peter Lambert; des. Sally Jay; with Jessie Evans, Robert
  Stephens as Dunois, Jeremy Brett as Ladvenu); Fortune Th., 17 Sept.
  1956 (solo performance by Nel Oosthout); Old Vic Th., 9 Feb. 1960
  (dir. Douglas Seale; des. Leslie Hurry; with Barbara Jefford, Alec
  McCowen, Robert Harris); National Th. at Chichester Festival Th.,
  24 June 1963 (dir. John Dexter; des. Michael Annals; with Joan
  Plowright, Robert Stephens, and Max Adrian), trans. Old Vic Th.,
  30 Oct. 1963; Mermaid Th., 3 Sept. 1970 (dir. Bernard Miles;
  des. Bryan Graves; with Angela Pleasence); Abbey Th., Dublin,
  5 Dec. 1972; Prospect Theatre Company at Old Vic Th.,
  4 May 1977 (dir. John Dove; des. Robin Archer; with Eileen Atkins,
  Charles Kay, Robert Eddison), revived Old Vic Th., 9 Feb. 1978

(with some changes of cast), revived Malvern Festival Th.,
Aug. 1978; National Th. at Olivier, 16 Feb. 1984 (dir. Ronald Eyre;
des. John Gunter; with Frances de la Tour, Cyril Cusack as the
Inquisitor, Michael Bryant as Cauchon, Philip Locke as
de Stogumber).
First published: in German, in serialized form, 1924.
First published in English: London: Constable, 1924.

---

*Successive episodes from the historical story of Joan of Arc
reveal her common sense and faith in her own perceptions and
intuitions, but also her unawareness of the minefield of subtle
political forces she moves through. In the debate between the
feudal power and the Catholic Church, and the theological
niceties of Joan's subsequent trial, are mirrored the twentieth-
century concepts of nationalism and protestantism. Twenty-five
years after Joan's execution, the principal characters visit the
Dauphin (now King) in a dream, and the matter of the play is set
in a different perspective.*

I have never been in Orleans before. ... I shall do a Joan play some day,
beginning with the sweeping up of the cinders and orange peel *after* her
martyrdom, and going on with Joan's arrival in heaven.

> Shaw, to Mrs. Patrick Campbell, 8 Sept. 1913,
> *Collected Letters*, 3, p. 201

The scenes in *Joan* can all be reduced to extreme simplicity. A single
pillar of the Gordon Craig type will make the cathedral. All the Loire
needs is a horizon and a few of Simonson's lanterns. The trial scene is as
easy as the cathedral. The others present no difficulty. There should be
an interval at the end of the Loire scene and one (very short) after the
trial sene, and even that makes an interval too many: the act divisions
should be entirely disregarded.

> Shaw, to Laurence Langner, 1923, quoted in
> Langner, *The Magic Curtain*, p. 175

The pictures have arrived. I had a long letter from Simonson ... about it.
On the whole there is nothing to complain of, which is a pity, as I
complain so well. ... The altar and candles in the middle of the cathedral
are feebly stagey, and do not give the effect of a corner of a gigantic

cathedral as my notion of one big pillar would. And it leads to that upstage effect, with a very feminine operatic looking Joan in the centre, which I wanted to avoid.

Shaw, to Lawrence Langner, 1 Feb. 1924,
Collected Letters, 3, p. 863

The Dauphin was beautifully played by Mr. Thesiger, who showed beneath his astonishing grotesqueries the pity and pathos of all weakness. ... There is a faintly jovial, quasi-satirical, and wholly unnecessary epilogue, conceived in a vein of lesser exultation. ... There is not an ounce of sensation anywhere in this piece, and the epilogue is implicit in all that has gone before. It is the greatest compliment to this play to say that at its tragic climax every eye was dry, so over-whelmingly had its philosophic import mastered sentiment. None in the audience would have saved Joan, even if he could.

The production was beyond all praise. ... The scenery, designed by Mr. Charles Ricketts, was neither frankly representational nor uncom-promisingly expressionistic, but a happy blend of the two. ... The dresses made a kind of music in the air, and at the end Joan was allowed to stand for a moment in all that ecstasy of tinsel and blue in which French image-makers enshrine her memory. ... Joan was excellent, boyish, brusque, inspired, exalted, mannerless, tactless, and obviously, once she had served her turn, a nuisance to everybody. The part is one which no actress who is leading lady only and not artist would look at. But Miss Thorndike is a noble artist, and did nobly.

James Agate, *Sunday Times*, 30 Mar. 1924,
reprinted in *Red Letter Nights*, p. 215-18

This is the first of his plays into which Shaw's senility creeps. The jokes misfire; the debates languish; and Shaw's passion for penal reform obtrudes to the detriment of the end. ... A divinely illuminated simple-ton, [Joan] is incapable of change or development. Or so it seems on the page. And this is where Siobhan McKenna comes in. ... This actress lets us see life stripping Joan down to her spiritual buff. The beaming clown of the opening scenes has undergone, by the end, an annealing: all that was mortal about her is peeled away, and sheer soul bursts through. 'God is alone' had tears flowing everywhere in the house, and during the epilogue one scarcely dared look at the stage.

Kenneth Tynan, on Arts Th. production (1954),
reprinted in *Curtains*, p. 83

How could this dreadful play, made up of heavy sentimentality, school-master's jokes, legal argument, and a baffling ignorance of the nature of sanctity — how could this bullying ramshackle bore of a play not only have held its place in the repertory, but still be regarded as a twentieth-century masterpiece and held to contain the greatest part written for an actress in this century? ...

The best scene in the play, the trial, has Shaw writing at his poor best. The immensely long but intellectually thrilling speech by the Inquisitor on the nature of heresy has been mercifully cut and is delivered with Robert Eddison's familiar pellucid gravity. ... Again Eileen Atkins triumphs. It is a wonder to see the gradual dawning ... that perhaps her voices have deceived her. It is the desolation of doubt in someone whose very substance is faith. Even more remarkable is the way she conveys her fear of incarceration, as if a spirit has been made aware of flesh in the most terrible way. She shakes and buckles as if caught in a slow-motion epileptic fit. Her eyes become Black Holes of terror. Great acting.

Julian Jebb, *Plays and Players*, July 1977, p. 30

The Apple Cart

A political extravaganza in two acts and an interlude.
Written: 1929.
First production: in Polish, Teatr Polski, Warsaw, 14 June 1929
(dir. Karel Borowski; des. Karol Frycz).
First English production: Malvern Festival Th., 19 Aug. 1929
(dir. H. K. Ayliff; des. Paul Shelving; with Cedric Hardwicke and
Edith Evans), trans. Queen's Th., London, 17 Sept. 1929.
First US production: Theatre Guild, Martin Beck Th., New York,
24 Feb. 1930.
Revived: Garrick Th., Melbourne, 9 Oct. 1933 (dir. Gregan McMahon,
who also played Magnus, with Coral Browne as Orinthia);
Cambridge Th., 25 Sept. 1935 (dir. Cedric Hardwicke; with Esmé
Percy); Arts Th., 7 Aug. 1946 (dir. Jack Hawkins, who also played
Magnus, and Peter Streuli; des. Fanny Taylor); Bedford Th., Camden
Town, 20 June 1949 (dir. Douglas Seale); Haymarket Th.,
7 May 1953 (dir. Michael MacOwan; des. Loudon Sainthill; with
Noël Coward, Margaret Leighton as Orinthia, and Margaret Rawlings
as Lysistrata); Arts Th., Cambridge, 1 June 1965 (dir. Peter Dews;
des. Hutchinson Scott; with Marius Goring); Chichester Festival Th.,
26 July 1977 (dir. Patrick Garland; des. Eileen Diss and
Raymond Hughes; with Keith Michell, Penelope Keith as Orinthia,

and Nigel Stock as Proteus); Haymarket Th., 20 Feb. 1986
(dir. Val May; des. Alexander MacPherson; with Peter O'Toole,
Susannah York, and Dora Bryan as Amanda).
First published: in German, 1929.
First published in English: in *Saint Joan, The Apple Cart* , London:
Constable, 1930 (*The Works*, Limited Edition, Vol 17).

---

*The royal secretaries' talk introduces the theme of royalty and
the politics of this imaginary future kingdom. Boanerges, who
represents trade union power, arives ahead of the rest of the
cabinet for a presentation to King Magnus. The Prime Minister
and the King play out the routine political game of con-
stitutional crisis. During an interlude, Magnus's equilibrium is
upset in the embrace of Orinthia, the royal mistress. While he is
taking tea with Queen Jemima, the American Ambassador
arrives to announce that his country is rejoining the British
Empire. The reassembled cabinet fails to grasp the genuine
crisis threatened by this polite form of annexation.*

The Apple Cart, which is as disconnected as a revue, is not, of course, a
play, but who cares whether it is or not? ... It opens with a discourse on
ritualism which has as much relevance to the rest of the play as the old-
fashioned overture had to the rest of the opera.

This discourse is added to the play in exactly the same spirit in which
the gargoyles were added to cathedrals, out of sheer exuberance and
overflow of genius. The second act is almost an independent piece, and
might, with little alteration, be performed by itself. The end is more or
less in the air. But what an entertainment!

St. John Ervine, The Observer, 25 Aug. 1929,
quoted in Barry Jackson and the London Theatre, p. 117

The main oversight in the criticism of *The Apple Cart* is the failure to
grasp the significance of the fact that the King wins, not *qua* King, but
qua potential Commoner. The tearing up of the ultimatum is almost
a defeat for him. It is certainly a defeat for Lysistrata (the Power
Mistress), whose depression the King shares when the shouting is over.

Shaw, The Observer, 1929, quoted in
Barry Jackson and the London Theatre, p. 118

At the Mermaid, ... *The Apple Cart* was staged in an elegant but curiously motionless and radio-like production. ... John Neville's Magnus was an urbane reminder of the Duke of Windsor in his pre-abdication days and the play itself ... emerged as an eerie fore-shadowing of the shape of things to come just seven years later. But, first impression to the contrary, *The Apple Cart* is not really about royalty in conflict with the workings of democratic government; rather it is about the financial tyranny of big business. ...

Sheridan Morley, *Review Copies*, p. 27

Seeing the Chichester Festival production of *The Apple Cart*, which came for a season to the Phoenix Theatre, I felt that if only he were not so cosily playful, ... you could still accept this work as a serious dialogue about the need for monarchy within a democracy and the superiority of personalities to institutions. ... Only in the interlude with Orinthia, ... incarnated by Penelope Keith, did the play prove really durable.

Anthony Curtis, *Drama*, No. 127, Winter 1977-78, p. 52

'The whole affair is a frightful bag of old stage tricks', said Shaw. 'I blushed when I saw it.' Some sparkle remains in his attack on uncaring plutocracy or democracy as 'the tyranny of popular ignorance', and on those who would sell Britain to the USA. Otherwise one comes out agreeing with GBS, who here has been further reduced to a star's minion.

John Barber, *Daily Telegraph*, 22 Feb. 1986

Too True to Be Good

Written: 1932.

First US production: Theatre Guild, National Th., Boston, Mass.,
  29 Feb. 1932 (dir. Leslie Banks; des. Jonel Jorgulesco; with
  Beatrice Lillie, Hugh Sinclair, Claude Rains), trans. Guild Th.,
  New York, 4 Apr. 1932.

First English production: Malvern Festival Th., 6 Aug. 1932
  (dir. H. K. Ayliff; des. Paul Shelving; with Ellen Pollock, Cedric
  Hardwicke, Ernest Thesiger, Ralph Richardson).

First London production: New Th., 13 Sept. 1932 (trans. from Malvern
  Festival).

Revived: Lyric Th., Hammersmith, 31 Oct. 1944 (dir. Ellen Pollock,
who played the Nurse; des. Riette Sturge Moore; with Margaret
Halstan, Michael Golden, Richard Goolden); Arts Th., 13 July 1948
(dir. Esmé Percy; with Marius Goring and Lucie Mannheim);
Pitlochry Festival Th., 21 May 1952 (dir. James Hume); Lyceum Th.,
Edinburgh, 6 Sept. 1965 (dir. Frank Dunlop; des. Tom Lingwood;
with Dora Bryan, Kenneth Haigh, Athene Seyler, Alastair Sim, James
Bolam, George Cole), trans. Strand Th., London, 22 Sept. 1965;
Riverside Studios, 5 Nov. 1986 (Shared Experience, dir. Mike
Alfreds; des. Paul Dart).
First published: in German, 1932; in Italian, 1933.
First published in English: in *Too True to Be Good, Village Wooing,
and On the Rocks*, London: Constable, 1934.

*The sick-bed of an ailing young woman, over-protected by a
fussy mother, is the setting for the prologue to the main action, a
microbe acting as chorus. The Patient connives with a Burglar,
let in by the Nurse, to steal her own necklace and escape to find
'real' life. The next setting for the fantasy is a beach somewhere
in the British Empire, where the three criminals live as idle rich
folk under the protection of Colonel Tallboys and his efficient
factotum, Private Meek. Characters, incidents, relationships
show the mixture of reality and absurdity which characterizes
dreams. This dream mirrors the disintegration of pre-war
certainties, morals and manners, not least the undermining of a
stable world-view by Freud and psychoanalysis. The play passes
from negative to positive when Mrs. Mopply (the Patient's
mother), in search of her daughter, so irritates the Colonel that
he thwacks her with an umbrella. This restores her to her senses
as a responsible human being, and mother and daughter enter
on a new alliance as equal and independent women. Sweetie, the
Nurse, finds her destiny in marriage to the puritanical Sergeant.
Aubrey, the Burglar, accepts that it is his nature to preach — an
inheritance from his father, the minatory Elder — though he is
lost in the mists, with no revelation to communicate.*

I know my business as a playwright too well to fall into the common
mistake of believing that because it is pleasant to be kept laughing for an
hour, it must be trebly pleasant to be kept laughing for three hours.
When people have laughed for an hour, they want to be serio-comically

entertained for the next hour; and when that is over they are so tired of not being wholly serious that they can bear nothing but a torrent of sermons.

My play is arranged accordingly.

Shaw, in *Malvern Festival Book*, 1932, p. 216-17

At the Lyric, Hammersmith, ... Shaw breaks all the rules of the theatre, yet none can be said to break them more successfully. In the first act we were introduced to the chief characters, but at curtain-fall Richard Goolden, as The Germ, told the audience that although the play was now virtually over the characters would resume the stage for the next two acts for the purpose of a discussion. ... However, the resultant conversation was so stimulating that one soon forgot the lack of plot and the unconventional construction and revelled in the wit of the Irish master.

Peter Noble, *British Theatre*, British Yearbooks, 1946, p. 140-1

This is a good deal more than a star production of a minor Shaw play. It is a well calculated act of revaluation designed to open up his neglected last phase. ...

It has become customary to regard everything he wrote after *The Apple Cart* in terms of senile decline: *Too True to be Good* (1931) follows that play by three years and far from suggesting waning powers shows that at the age of 75 he had the energy to embark on a new genre fitted to the task of 'foreseeing and being prepared for realities as yet unexperienced'.

The preoccupations of the play are related at every point to those of today — patriotic disenchantment, affluent youth, experimental morality, and a sense of impending catastrophe. Another relationship is Shaw's choice of anarchic comedy to express his vision of humanity on the edge of the abyss, regarding it — like our own practitioners of the absurd — as a prospect too dreadful to be taken seriously. ... In the figure of his spokesman, the burglar-preacher ... one sees Shaw stripping himself as well as his victims to the bone.

For those who have heard the play described as disjointed and incoherent it is a surprise to discover it to be clearly articulated. ... What holds it together is the logic of the adventure. Miss Mopply sells her jewelry abetted by the burglar and his accomplice Sweetie, and they take off to conduct an experiment in happiness — an experiment that fails dismally, but the presence of disenchanted older figures ... makes it plain that they too are lost creatures and that the experiment was worth making.

Irving Wardle, *The Times*, 7 Sept. 1965

It must be one of the most oddly-constructed pieces ever written by a major dramatist, but Shaw knew far too much about dramatic architecture to have arrived at its bizarrre shape by accident or clumsiness. ... Mr. Williams appears to have given up hope of imposing any unity. ... And the physical decoration in scenery and costume sometimes perversely neglects the guidance Shaw has been able to give. ... Mr. Koltai ... has constructed plastic towers, totally lacking in realistic relevance, which give the impression that we have strayed into the world of *Dr. Who*. ...

It was [Shaw's] ability to understand what was happening at the time which was extraordinary. If he seems to be foreseeing our future, it is because history is repeating itself. ... What is true, but not good ... is that the messages are buried under rather stale stage tricks, familiar devices and old jokes ...

Alan Brien, *Plays and Players*, Dec. 1975, p. 22-3

Village Wooing

'A comediettina' for two voices in three conversations.
Written: 1933.
First US production: Little Th., Dallas, 16 Apr. 1934 (dir. Charles
    Meredith, who also played 'A', with Keith Woolley as 'Z').
First English production: Pump Room, Tunbridge Wells
    (dir. Christopher Fry, who played 'A'; des. Ian Seraillier; with Eileen
    Midwood as 'Z').
First London production: Little Th., 19 June 1934 (dir. Shaw;
    des. Yootha Rose; with Arthur Wontner as 'A', Sybil Thorndike as
    'Z').
Revived: Abbey Th., Dublin, 30 Sept. 1935; Torch Th., 10 Jan. 1939
    (dir. Stewart Granger; des. G. R. Schjelderup; with Ellen Pollock and
    Robert Adam); Arts Th., 1 Dec. 1942 (dir. Stanford Holme; with
    Joan Hickson and Walter Hudd); Lyric Th., Hamersmith,
    28 Nov. 1944 (dir. Ellen Pollock, who also played 'Z';
    des. Riette Sturge Moore); New Lindsay Th., 27 Aug. 1946 (dir. Peter
    Cotes); Lyric Th., Hammersmith, 2 Aug. 1949 (dir. Richard Wadleigh
    and Jon Penington); Arts Th., 20 June 1951 (dir. Roy Rich; with
    Brenda Bruce and Maurice Denham); Royal Court Th., 26 July 1952
    (dir. Ellen Pollock, who also played 'Z'); Lyceum Th., Edinburgh,
    3 Sept. 1956 (dir. Roy Rich; with Brenda Bruce and
    Michael Denison); Mermaid Th., 1965; Fortune Th., 26 Jan. 1970
    (dir. Nigel Patrick; des. Motley; with Dulcie Gray and
    Michael Denison); Th. at New End, Hampstead, 8 Oct. 1981

(dir. Frank Hauser; des. Nick Ormerod; with Judi Dench and Michael
Williams); with *Overrruled*, Theatre Museum, London, 29 Jan 1989.
First published: in *Too True to Be Good, Village Wooing, and On the
Rocks*, London: Constable, 1934.

*A telephonist's chatter interrupts the work of a travel writer on
a cruise. In the second part, they meet again in her village store
and make a match of it.*

One critic, commenting on a recording I did of *A Village Wooing*, said
that when I play Shaw, I give him heart. This is not true — his heart is
there, big as anything. Two speeches ... on the relation of man and
woman are intensely poetic and moving.

Siobhan McKenna, *Theatre Arts*, Mar. 1957

The piece is a devastatingly economic analysis of an awkward com-
panionship progressing through materialistic partnership (as the writer
acquires the family post office) and uneasy romance. It is played quite
beautifully. ... The final punch line should be more emphatically iso-
lated: it is, after all, the play's best joke that neither party knows the
other's name.

Michael Coveney, *Financial Times*, 9 Oct. 1981

On the Rocks

A political comedy in two acts.
Written: 1933.
First production: Winter Garden Th., 25 Nov. 1933 (dir. Lewis Casson;
des. Peter Bax; with Nicholas Hannen, Ellen Pollock as Aloysia,
Edward Rigby as Hipney).
First US production: Daly's Th., New York, 15 June 1938.
Revived: Abbey Th., Dublin, 9 July 1934; Malvern Festival Th., 27 July
1936 (dir. Herbert M. Prentice; des. Jean Campbell; with Stephen
Murray and Elspeth March); Pitlochry Festival Th., 21 Apr. 1967
(dir. Michael Barry; des. Kenneth Bridgeman; with Michael Forrest
as Chavender, Will Leighton as Hipney); Mermaid Th., 21 Aug. 1975
(dir. Bernard Miles, who played Hipney; des. Bernard Culshaw; with
Stephen Murray as Chavender); Chichester Festival Th., 5 May 1982

(dir. Patrick Garland and Jack Emery; des. Pamela Howard; with
Keith Michell as Chavender, Arthur English as Hipney).
First published: in *Too True to Be Good, Village Wooing, and On the
Rocks*, London: Constable, 1934.

*The play is set in the cabinet room, 10 Downing Street. The
Prime Minister, Sir Arthur Chavender, is in a state of break-
down, and is advised by a Lady Doctor to go into her clinic-
retreat. A deputation from the Isle of Cats (a comic chorus)
prompts him to take the classic texts of socialism with him. On
his return, a new man, he proposes a coherent socialist policy to
his cabinet; but his attempt to unite them fails. The comic
deputation returns, and its senior member, Alderman Hipney,
voices his own political disillusionment and (a devil's advocate)
urges Chavender to adopt the fascist solution. Instead, the
Prime Minister writes his letter of resignation, and the unemployed march into Downing Street.*

It has been said that this is a 'fascist' play. That, I think, mistakes
Mr. Shaw's intention. It warns rather than advocates. Make up your
mind, he says, that Parliament, as you now know it, cannot be the
instrument of salvation.

Kingsley Martin,
New Statesman and Nation, 2 Dec. 1933

The final revised version ... was sent to you a few days ago. The most
important change in the dialogue is the omission of the letter of
resignation to the King, which I discarded after the first performance.
The changes in stage business are considerable. ... You suggest
Mrs. Baker-Eddy as a future heroine. But she is in *On the Rocks* as the
Lady Doctor.

Shaw, to Siegfried Trebitsch, 22 Dec. 1933,
Bernard Shaw's Letters to Siegfried Trebitsch, ed. Samuel A. Weiss,
Stanford University Press, 1986, p. 339

Once Chavender returns from Wales ... the play ends up on the rocks
itself: the broad but lively antics of Act One are swept aside and we are
faced with the meat of the matter — talk, talk, talk. ...

The play's director, Bernard Miles, ... puts in two telling appearances as ... Hipney, a veteran of eleven deputations of the unemployed. 'Don't mind me, sir, I don't matter!' he says, only to scene-steal outrageously with his chats to Chavender, full of crusty home truths ... interspersed with tight little laughs and nervous waves of his hand-held hat.

Geoff Brown, *Plays and Players*, Oct. 1975, p. 39

It seems to me precisely the sort of thing decent people should *not* have resurrected at a time like this, when unemployment is once again rife, party alignments confused, and parliamentary democracy itself under attack from both right and left.

Benedict Nightingale, *New Statesman*, 14 May 1982

One salutes Shaw's humanitarian response, but it torpedoes the play.

However, it is imagination, not senility, that scuppers the plot. *On The Rocks* ... shows his anarchic comic gift doing spirited battle with his authoritarian opinions: and the separate factions are orchestrated with effortless fluency and the ability to spring surprises. ...

Keith Michell plays Chavender ... as a political matinee idol. ... It lets him down after the Marxist change of heart, particularly when confronted by Aubrey Woods's grim police chief and Arthur English as the old forelock-tugging revolutionist Hipney — a part calculated to steal every scene he gets and played here with a wry conviction that goes far beyond the comic boundaries.

Irving Wardle, *The Times*, 6 May 1982, p. 15

The Simpleton of the Unexpected Isles

A play in a prologue and two acts.
Written: 1934.
First production: Theatre Guild, Guild Th., New York, 18 Feb. 1935 (dir. Henry Wagstaffe Gribble; des. Lee Simonson; with Nazimova as Prola).
First English production: Malvern Festival Th., 29 July 1935 (dir. Herbert Prentis; des. Marion Spencer; with Vivienne Bennett, Cecil Trouncer, Stephen Murray, Elspeth March).
First Australian production: Comedy Th., Melbourne, Oct. 1935 (dir. Gregan McMahon).
First London production: Arts Th., 7 Mar. 1945 (dir. Judith Furse; des. Michael Warre; with Mark Dignam and Peter Jones).

Revived: Manchester Green Room, 30 Jan. 1953; Shaw Festival,
 Niagara-on-the-Lake, June 1983 (dir. Denise Coffey).
First published: in German, 1935.
First published in English: in *The Simpleton, The Six, and The
 Millionairess*, London: Constable, 1936.

*This is a utopian fable to end utopianism. A young woman
without papers arrives at an outpost of Empire and persuades
the Emigration Officer to show her round the island. They meet
a priest and a priestess, Pra and Prola, who purge them by
immersion in the sea. While the four are sharing a vegetarian
meal, two other tourists, Mr. and Mrs. Farwaters, arrive
separately and succumb to the attractiveness of Prola and Pra.
Twenty years later, a naive English clergyman ('Iddy'), put
ashore by pirates, comes across the colony founded by the
group marriage of the six who gathered in the prologue. Iddy
mistakes their children for divine images. Their parents are
aware of having bred beautiful illusions and hope, by bringing
Iddy into the family, to introduce an element of moral conscience. This experiment, in turn, is unsuccessful and is ended,
in Act II, by the Day of Judgement announced by a matter-of-
fact Angel. The beautiful children, being empty ideals, vanish,
as idle and worthless people are reported to be vanishing from
all parts of the British Empire. The older generation goes back
to work and Iddy, released, sets out to find his English village
again.*

Almost a Shavian revue, purporting to debunk love, hate, patriotism,
religion, eugenics, dietetics, war, and imperialism ... a magnificent
confusion.

The Bulletin, Sydney, 16 Oct. 1935

This Shavian vision of Judgement is new to the London stage. ... Its
neglect is not perhaps so shocking as might appear. ... The piece — a
slow-moving serio-comic allegory with a poetic finale which seems to
break upon Mr. Shaw unexpectedly — lacks narrative clearness. It is
amusing in parts, and the audience feels itself to be peering through
clouds of farcical incident and satirical comment ... for the general outline of the mountains, for the meaning of the allegory. ... Mr. Peter

Jones lends the simpleton clergyman amiability, and Mr. Bill Shine makes good fun of the unexpectedly fussy angel.

The Times, 8 Mar. 1945

The situation, with its several dubiously happy couples, is vaguely reminiscent of a Shakespearian romance. ... Can [the company] make this pastiche palatable? Amazingly, yes. ... There is ... a cerain amount of fun about the uncanny foresight of the play, which could be set inside any hippy ashram of a decade ago (Beatles music drops the hint). There is also Denise Coffey's remarkable staging ... happily mating everything from vaudeville turns to anguished soliloquies in a graceful and finely tuned production.

Ray Conlogue, *Globe and Mail*, Toronto, 1 July 1983

It was the Falklands war that triggered [Denise Coffey's] interest in *Simpleton*, which features in its bizarre plot the arrival of fleets from all over the British Empire to threaten battle over a tiny island. ... This cheerful mess now has more vitality than the oppressively well-constructed *Candida*. ... *Simpleton* gleefully lampoons the sort of crackpot Victorian reform Shaw himself so often seemed to personify.

Martin Knelman, *Saturday Night*,
Toronto, XCVIII, No. 9, Sept. 1983

The Millionairess

A 'Jonsonian comedy' in four acts.
Written: 1935.
First production: in German, Akademie Theater, Vienna, 4 Jan. 1936
    (dir. Herbert Wanick; des. Willi Bahner; with Maria Eis).
First English-language production: McMahon Players, King's Th.,
    Melbourne, Australia, 7 Mar. 1936 (dir. Gregan MacMahon; with
    Enid Hollins).
First English production: Matthew Forsyth Repertory Company,
    De La Warre Pavilion, Bexhill-on-Sea, 17 Nov. 1936.
First US production: Country Playhouse, Westport, Conn.
    (prod. Lawrence Langner and Armina Marshall).
Revived: Malvern Festival Th., 26 July 1937 (dir. Herbert M. Prentice;
    des. Marion Spencer; with Elspeth March); Devonshire Ark Th.,
    Eastbourne, 22 Jan. 1940 (dir. Leon M. Lion; with Sara Tapping, for
    whom Shaw adapted leading role to suit a judo expert); pre-London
    tour organized by H. M. Tennant, prevented by the Blitz from
    opening at Globe Th., 11 Sept. 1940 (dir. George Devine; des.

Ruth Keating; with Edith Evans); 'Q' Th., 29 May 1944
(dir. Geoffrey Wardwell; des. Elizabeth Agombar; with Phyllis
Neilson-Terry and Frederick Valk).

First West End production: New Th., 27 June 1952 (dir. Michael
Benthall; des. James Bailey; with Katherine Hepburn, Robert
Helpmann, Cyril Ritchard), trans. Shubert Th., New York, 17 Oct.
1952.

Revived: Haymarket Th., 14 Dec. 1978 (dir. Michael Lindsay-Hogg;
des. Alan Tagg and Robin Fraser Paye; with Penelope Keith, Charles
Kay, Ian Ogilvy, Nigel Hawthorne); Greenwich Th., 10 Oct. 1988
(dir. Penny Cherns; des. Douglas Heap; with Barbara Flynn).

Film: Twentieth Century Fox, 1960 (dir. Antony Asquith; with
Sophia Loren and Peter Sellers).

First published: in German, 1935.

First published in English: in *The Simpleton, The Six, and The
Millionairess*, London: Constable, 1936.

---

*This farcical drama on the theme of capitalism opens with
Epifania, 'a plutocrat of the plutocrats', requiring her solicitor
to draw up her will before she commits suicide from shame at a
diminution of her income, and revulsion from her marriage
to an unsatisfactory husband. Coincidentally, Alastair, the
husband, turns up wanting a divorce. His account of how he
made the large sum Epifania's father demanded is a comic
lesson in economics. In Act II, set in a riverside inn, Eppy
throws Adrian, her lover, downstairs for criticizing her father.
The noise brings in an Egyptian doctor, with whom she instantly
falls in love. Like Eppy's father, the doctor's mother devised a
test for anyone he might consider marrying, and Epifania
accepts the terms of having to earn her own living for six
months with only thirty-five shillings to start her on her way.
Act III shows her working in a sweat shop, then taking over the
organization of the business and turning out the original
owners. All the principal characters turn up at the former inn,
now transformed into a first-class hotel, and the ruthless money-
maker claims the Mohammedan servant of others as her mate.*

The sweater and his wife speak Whitechapel Cockney. ... The pair
would ordinarily be Jews; but you must carefully avoid any suggestion
of this at present, as it would drag in current politics. ...

The woman's quiet cryng must give a hopeless pathos to the end of the scene. ... There is not a gleam of fun in these two poor devils.

Shaw, to Matthew Forsyth, 1936, quoted in
Mander and Mitchenson, <i>Theatrical Companion to Shaw</i>, p. 248-9

Less preaching and dogmatizing ... than in anything Shaw has written for ten years. ... A curious third act, of short duration, in which employers of sweated labour are flagellated in the Upton Sinclair manner, ... [The fourth act is] superb comedy — impudent, pungent, and devastating ... he has kept the best for the last.

The Argus, Melbourne, 8 Mar. 1936

The Millionairess, with Edith Evans in the title part, is next on the list at the Globe Theatre in London. In the original version I made the woman a boxer; but, on the stage [*at Malvern*], that was unconvincing and unladylike. So I have made her a Judo expert. Judo is what we vulgarly call jujitsu, which is magnificently spectacular. The part requires just such a personality as Miss Hepburn. Has she ever read the play?

Shaw, to Lawrence Langner, 3 Apr. 1940, in Langner,
The Magic Curtain, Harrap, 1952, p. 411

The central character is quite hateful. Epifania, described by Shaw as a born boss, bangs through the play like a battering ram, living at the top of her lungs, and barking orders like a games mistress run amok. There is something of a crowbar about her charm, and something, too, of a rhinoceros.

The part is nearly unactable; yet Miss Hepburn took it, acted it, and found a triumph in it. She glittered like a bracelet thrown up at the sun; she was metallic, yet reminded us that metals shine and can also melt. Epifania clove to her ... and from first word to last, star and part are treading common ground. ... As I could have predicted, she was stark, staring, and scandalously bold, alternately shooting the lines point-blank at us and brandishing them like flags. ... What is astonishing about her is her warmth. Her grins gleam at you; and as she shapes them, she droops the corners of her eyelids and twinkles like a fire. And in her last long speech, a defence of marriage and all the risks it implies, ... James Bailey's plushy setting disappeared from my mind. ...

The supporting cast had done much valiant and loving work. Robert Helpmann, rakish under a tarboosh, had padded pop-eyed through the role of the Egyptian doctor and made it eloquent. Cyril Ritchard had lent a flustered dignity, like that of a goosed hen, to the nonentity Blenderbland. But they vanished then, and it was, as it had been meant to be, Miss Hepburn's night.

> Kenneth Tynan, on performance in Coventry, 1952,
> in *The Observer*, reprinted in *Curtains*, p. 27-8

Geneva

'A fancied page of history' in three acts.
Written: 1938.
First production: Malvern Festival Th., 1 Aug. 1938 (dir. H. K. Ayliff; des. Paul Shelving; with Donald Wolfit, Ernest Thesiger, Cecil Trouncer, Norman Wooland), trans. Saville Th., London, 22 Nov. 1938, trans. St. James's Th., 27 Jan. 1939.
First US production: Henry Miller's Th., New York, 30 Jan. 1940 (Colbourne-Jones Company).
Revived: Comedy Th., Melbourne, 10 July 1939 (dir. Gregan McMahon); Mermaid Th., 4 Nov. 1971 (dir. Philip Grout; des. John Halle and Mary Moore).
First published: with illustrations by Feliks Topolski, London: Constable, 1939; extended and updated edition, London: Constable, 1940.

This political cartoon in dramatic form opens in the small office of the Committee for International Co-operation. The Secretary, Begonia Brown, receives three successive visitors with complaints against the governments of their own countries. Finally, an English Bishop and a Russian Commissar both protest against foreign interference in the internal affairs of their respective lands. Act II, in the office of the Secretary of the League of Nations, introduces the British Foreign Secretary, carries forward the plot with accounts of the response to the warrants Begonia has sought from the International Court at the Hague, and brings on that young lady, announcing her decision to stand for Parliament. In Act III, the Court sits at the Hague: the ensemble of characters gathers, with the addition of Begonia's young man, a silly clown type. Those summoned do, in fact, appear: burlesque versions of Mussolini, Franco, and Hitler, drawn by the limelight, before the bar of public opinion and, ultimately, of Christianity — represented by an English

Deaconess. The play is brought to an end by a fantastic plot-device which sets the political wrangles in a new perspective.

Newcomer is a bother. ... Ein alt (or echt) Radikal might do, if Radicalism means what it does in England ... an old-fashioned supporter of what used to be the extreme left of Liberalism.

> Shaw, to his translator, Siegfried Trebitsch, 5 Aug. 1938,
> *Shaw's Letters to Siegfried Trebitsch*, p. 375

The first two acts of this play were written long before the third, are far more frankly farcical, and serve as mere anti-chambers to the final court of justice. They are much less urgent and important in their matter, though full of quips and definitions that have the lighter Shavian ring. ... But the point and essence of *Geneva* is the very long third act, in which three easily recognizable trouble-makers ... are arrraigned for destroying the liberty of Europe. ... The judge ... dismisses the court at the end, and with it the wrangling world it represents. ... We are a hopeless world, and man as a political animal is a total failure. Mr. Shaw ... is here seen and heard washing his hands of us; and he uses a good disinfectant soap and the coldest clear water in doing so.

> Alan Dent, *The Spectator*, 5 Aug. 1938

In *John Bull's Other Island*, I ... have been far less kind to the Irish characters than I have been to the Jew in *Geneva*, who is introduced solely to convict the Nazis of persecution. But you will not allow him to do exactly what an able Jew of his type would do when Gentiles were swallowing a terrifying press canard: that is, go into the moneymarket as a bear speculator and make his fortune. ...

However, to please you, I have written up the part a bit. Musso let me down completely by going anti-Semite on me; and I have had to revise the third act to such an extent that you may now put the copy I sent you in the fire as useless.

> Shaw, to Lawrence Langner, 20 Sept. 1938,
> quoted in *GBS and the Lunatic*, Hutchinson, 1961, p. 167-8

I have added a scene to *Geneva* including the declaration of war and the Russian intervention, which you must add to your translation.

> Shaw, to Siegfried Trebitsch, 22 Sept. 1939,
> *Shaw's Letters to Siegfried Trebitsch*, p. 389

Geneva ... is his fiftieth play. ... In this theatregoer's opinion it is dull. For all his agility of mind, Mr. Shaw, now 83 years of age, can make the intellect seem extraordinarily futile.

Brooks Atkinson,
New York Times, 31 Jan. 1940

The old man's impatient anarchy wore surprisingly well, despite one or two wincingly insensitive lines. ... Barbara Ferris is ... a splendid, plump middle-aged, cosy, managing Begonia Brown, the very voice of the *petit bourgeoisie*.

J. W. Lambert,
Drama, No. 104, Spring 1972, p. 27

In Good King Charles's Golden Days

'A True History that Never Happened.'
Written: 1938-39.
First production: Malvern Festival Th., 12 Aug. 1939 (dir. H. K. Ayliff; des. Paul Shelving; with Ernest Thesiger, Cecil Trouncer, Yvonne Arnaud, Eileen Beldon, Irene Vanburgh), trans. Streatham Hill Th., 15 Apr. 1940, then New Theatre, London, 9 May 1940.
First New York production: Downtown Th., 24 Jan. 1957.
Revived: Maddermarket Th., Norwich, Nov. 1939 (dir. Nugent Monck; with amateur cast); King's Th., Melbourne, 9 Dec. 1939 (dir. Gregan McMahon, who played the King); People's Palace, London, 25 Oct. 1948 (dir. Matthew Forsyth; des. Paul Shelving; with Ernest Thesiger); Malvern Festival Th., 11 Aug. 1949 (dir. Ernest Thesiger; who played the King; des. Paul Shelving); Malvern Festival Th., 1983.
First published: London: Constable, 1939.

Essentially a discussion play, in which the nature and exercise of power and leadership are debated between King Charles II, Isaac Newton (the voice of science), George Fox (the man of religion), and the Dutchman Kneller (who speaks as artist), with interventions from three of the King's mistresses and his rejected but regal Queen, Catherine of Braganza. There are incidental fisticuffs between Newton and the Duke of York.

I have submitted it to two famous astronomers with the result that I have had to make a budget of corrections.

> Shaw, to Siegfried Trebitsch, 13 July 1939,
> *Shaw's Letters to Siegfried Trebitsch*, p. 387

Mr. Shaw's new play, ... produced this afternoon at Malvern before a crowded house, and with enormous success, contains nothing to which the most conservative playgoer could refuse assent. ... Is this a good play? ... It depends entirely on the playgoer. If you find the perihelion of Mercury more interesting than the perimeter of Lady Castlemain. Yes. If not. No. For the ladies are but ornaments. ... Will anybody miss the lack of action? Yes, the witless and the idle. ...

Mr. Shaw can always be relied on for one purple passage. This play has at least ... two in each act. And the body and bulk of it is the best warp and woof that has come from the Shavian loom since *Methuselah*.

> James Agate, *Sunday Times*, 13 Aug. 1939

b: Minor Plays

Apart from posthumously published early works (including two acts of a *Passion Play* in verse and a dramatic adaptation for copyright purposes of Ethel Voynitch's anarchist romance, *The Gadfly*) and the last flickers of his art which followed *Buoyant Billions — Farfetched Fables* and the unfinished *Why She Would Not* — Shaw wrote a number of one-act plays, skits, curtain-raisers, a puppet play (*Shakes versus Shav*), a free adaptation of a full-length play in German by Siegfried Trebitsch (*Jitta's Atonement*), a new final act for Shakespeare's *Cymbeline* entitled *Cymbeline Refinished*, and other dialogues. Of the playlets he wrote for particular occasions, only *Interlude at the Playhouse* (written 1907 for Winifred Emery and Cyril Maude) has resisted revival. The one-act plays and burlesques have been performed oftener in provincial theatres and by amateurs than in the mainstream London theatre. Most work well on their own terms and merit brief mention below.

Passion, Poison and Petrifaction, or *The Fatal Gazogene*

A burlesque of melodrama in one act.
First production: Theatrical Garden Party, Regent's Park, 14 July 1905 (dir. Cyril Maude, who played Adolphus Bastable; with Irene Vanburgh, Eric Lewis, Nancy Price).
Radio version: 15 Jan 1928, the first play by Shaw to be broadcast.

Press Cuttings

A topical sketch in one act, 'compiled ... from the daily papers during the Woman's War'.
Written: 1909, but refused a licence for public performance.
First production: private performance by the Civic and Dramatic Guild, Court Th., 9 and 12 July 1909 (dir. Shaw; with Robert Loraine, Leon Quartermaine, Agnes Thomas).
First public production: Gaiety Th., Manchester, 27 Sept. 1909 (dir. B. Iden Payne).

The Fascinating Foundling

'A disgrace to the author' in one act.
Written: 1909, for Elizabeth Asquith (Princess Bibesco).

First production: for charity, 1909.
First professional production: Arts Th., 28 Jan. 1928 (dir. Henry Oscar; with Peggy Ashcroft).

The Glimpse of Reality

A 'tragedietta' in one act.
Written: 1909, for Granville Barker, but not produced until after its publication in 1926.
First production: by amateurs, Fellowship Hall, Glasgow, 8 Oct. 1927.
First professional production: Arts Th., 20 Nov. 1927 (dir. Maurice Browne; with Harcourt Williams and Elissa Landi).

Overruled

A 'demonstration' in one act.
Written: 1912.
First production: Duke of York's Th., 14 Oct. 1912 (dir. Shaw; with Miriam Lewes and Geraldine Oliffe). [Shaw claimed to have shown the sexual act on stage in this play, but the critics did not notice.]

Great Catherine

'A thumbnail sketch of Russian court life', in four scenes.
Written: 1913, and first published in German, 1914.
First production: Vaudeville Th., 18 Nov. 1913 (dir. Shaw; with Gertrude Kingston and Norman McKinnel).
Film version: Warner/Keep Films, 1968 (dir. Gordon Flemyng; with Jeanne Moreau, Zero Mostel, Peter O'Toole).

The Music-Cure

'A piece of utter nonsense' in one act.
Written: 1913, as a curtain-raiser to celebrate the hundredth performance of G. K. Chesterton's *Magic*.
First production: Little Th., 28 Jan. 1914 (dir. 'Everybody Concerned'; with William Armstrong, Frank Randall, Madge McIntosh).
Revived: Arts Th., 27 June 1951 (dir. John Fernald; with Brenda Bruce, Gerald Harper, Alan MacNaughtan).

The Inca of Perusalem

'A comedietta in one act.'
Written: 1916.
First production: Birmingham Repertory Th., 7 Oct. 1916 (dir. John
   Drinkwater; with Felix Aylmer, Gertrude Kingston, William
   Armstrong).
First public production in London: Bedford Th., Camden Town
   (dir. Douglas Seale).

Augustus Does His Bit

A farce in one act, or 'official dramatic tract on war saving and cognate
   topics'.
Written: 1916.
First production: Stage Society, Royal Court Th., 21 and 22 Jan. 1917
   (dir. Shaw).
First US production: by amateurs, Polio's Th., Washington, 10 and
   11 Dec. 1917.
First public professional production: Comedy Th., New York, 12 Mar.
   1919 (dir. Norman Trevor).
Revived: Arts Th., 20 June 1951 (dir. Roy Rich; with Alan
   MacNaughtan and Brenda Bruce).

Annajanska, the Bolshevik Empress

A 'romancelet' in one act.
Written: 1917, originally entitled *Annajanska, the Wild Duchess.*
First production: Coliseum Th., 21 Jan. 1918 (dir. Shaw; costume des.
   Charles Ricketts; with Lillah McCarthy and Randle Ayrton).
Revived: Torch Th., 10 Jan. 1939 (dir. Stewart Granger; with Elspeth
   March); Arts Th., 20 June 1951 (dir. John Fernald; with Rachel
   Gurney).

The Six of Calais

Play in one act
Written: 1934.
First production: Open Air Th., Regent's Park, 17 July 1934
   (dir. Maxwell Wray; des. J. Gower Parks; with Phyllis Neilson-Terry,
   Hubert Gregg, Charles Carson).

All the above plays and playlets, together with other known fugitive
dramatic pieces, are included in the Bodley Head edition of Shaw's
Plays, Volumes III-VII. In a slightly different category is Shaw's last
substantial full-length play:

Buoyant Billions

A comedy of no manners in four acts.
Written: 1946-48.
First production: in German, Schauspielhaus, Zurich, 21 Oct. 1948
(dir. Berthold Viertel; des. Teo Otto; with Maria Beck).
First English production: Malvern Festival Th., 13 Aug. 1949
(dir. Esmé Percy; des. Theodora Winsten; with Frances Day and
Denholm Elliott), trans. Princes Th., London, 10 Oct. 1949.
First published: in German, 1948; in English, London: Constable, 1949.

Shaw was famous as a writer before he completed his first stage piece; and its successors were enjoyed by critics (notably A. B. Walkley of *The Times*) who continued to insist that he was a brilliant journalist, but no playwright. His first published writings were 'ghostings' for G. T. Vandeleur Lee on musical topics, though his posthumously published juvenilia include an entirely unorthodox *Passion Play* in verse (in the Bodley Head edition of the *Plays*, Vol. VII) and the fictitious letters to a child, *My Dear Dorothea* (Phoenix House, 1956), inspired by George Augustus Sala's *Lady Chesterfield's Letters to Her Daughter*.

Novels

The novels Shaw wrote during his first years in London were 'loose, baggy monsters' in the nineteenth-century tradition, with long digressions, much variety of mood and tone, and tenuous plots worked out and changed quite freely in the writing. Although several publishers' readers commented on the odd, wide-ranging, lively mind and skilful pen at work, and one remarked that *Cashel Byron's Profession* was 'the most comical book I have ever read', getting the novels published was slow work. The first to be completed was given the title *Immaturity* for its first appearance in print in 1930 (*Works*, Limited Edition, Vol. I, then in Standard Edition); it might equally well have been called 'A Young Man's Discovery of London'.

Each of the other novels has a clearer unifying idea, stated in the title of *Love Among the Artists* (written 1881; first published 1900); marriage, in the context of scientific positivism, in *The Irrational Knot* (serialized in the socialist paper, *To-Day*, 1885-87); class barriers, individual genius, and the struggle for success in *Cashel Byron's Profession*, an adventure story about a prize-fighter and an heiress (written 1882; serialized in *To-Day*, 1885-86); and the dilemma of the revolutionary who has profited from the society he wants to change in *An Unsocial Socialist* (serialized in *To-Day*, 1884). Trefusis, the hero of this last, is driven, Hamlet-like, to put on 'an antic disposition', and much of the novel is concerned with his attempts to work through women, philandering with political ends. As a wealthy, revolutionary philosopher, he foreshadows Jack Tanner in *Man and Superman*. The sexual cat-and-mouse games recur in several plays, including *Pygmalion*.

These four novels were included, in revised form, in the Limited and Standard editions of Shaw's *Works* (London: Constable, 1930 and 1931 respectively). A sixth novel was begun, and the fragment has been published as *An Unfinished Novel*, edited by S. Weintraub (Constable, 1958).

Political Writings

These works might never have seen the light, had it not been for Shaw's political activities as a leading Fabian Socialist. He edited — and contributed to — *Fabian Essays in Socialism* (Fabian Society, 1889; Jubilee Edition, Allen and Unwin, 1948). He drafted manifestos and wrote tracts for the Fabian Society over a period stretching from 1884 to 1929, and these were collected, with some additions, as *Essays in Fabian Socialism* (*Works*, Standard Edition, 1931; Limited Edition, 1932). His popularity in England was destroyed for several years by *Common Sense about the War* (in *Works*, Limited Edition, 1930, Standard Edition, 1931). *How to Settle the Irish Question* (Dublin: Talbot Press, 1917) is included, with other speeches and writings, in *The Matter with Ireland*, ed. David H. Greene and Dan H. Laurence (Hart-Davies, 1962).

Other extensive political books were *The Intelligent Woman's Guide to Socialism and Capitalism* (Constable, 1928; expanded for Pelican Books, to include accounts of Fascism and Communism, 1937) and *Everybody's Political What's What?* (Constable, 1944), his final work of substance. The titles are blatantly populist, reflecting the author's democratic belief that nothing is beyond the understanding of the ordinary man or woman, if it is lucidly, directly, and penetratingly explained. Further collections, published posthumously, are *Platform and Pulpit*, lectures and speeches, 1885-1946, ed. Dan H. Laurence (Hart-Davis, 1961); *The Rationalization of Russia*, an abandoned fragment (Indiana University Press, 1964); and *Practical Politics*, ed. Lloyd J. Hubenka (University of Nebraska Press, 1976).

Critical Writings

Having started as an uncredited journalist-reviewer of books and paintings, Shaw made his first reputation as a music critic with articles for *The Star*, under the pseudonym of 'Corno di Bassetto'. He made it a rule to jettison academic jargon in order to disperse the false mystique isolating the arts from a general public. As G.B.S., he was the drama critic for *The Saturday Review*, 1895-98, having already expounded Ibsen for the Fabian Society as early as 1891. This apprenticeship familiarized the future playwright with a London theatre and repertoire he determined to change radically in Ibsen's wake. The following is a brief checklist of Shaw's critical writings:

The Quintessence of Ibsenism (1891; revised and extended, 1913).
The Perfect Wagnerite (1898).
The Sanity of Art (1895; in book form, 1908).
[These last three were collected together as *Major Critical Essays* (*Works*, Limited Edition, 1930, Standard Edition, 1931; there is also a Penguin edition, ed. Michael Holroyd.]
Dramatic Opinions and Essays, two volumes of collected *Saturday Review* articles (1906).
Our Theatres in the Nineties, in three volumes, with 38 essays added to those in *Dramatic Opinions* (*Works*, Limited Edition, 1930; Standard Edition, 1931).
London Music in 1888-89, mainly articles from *The Star* (*Works,* 1937).
How to Become a Musical Critic, uncollected writings from 1876 to 1950 (Hart-Davis, 1961).
[These last three, together with *The Perfect Wagnerite* and further uncollected items, were brought together in three volumes of the Bodley Head Shaw, as *Music* (Reinhardt, 1981).]
Pen Portraits and Reviews, from various sources, 1892-1927 (*Works*, Limited and Standard Editions, 1931).
Non-Dramatic Literary Criticism, posthumously collected.

Miscellaneous Prose

Among the essays written by Shaw on miscellaneous subjects, the best-known appear as prefaces to most published editions of Shaw's plays. These were gathered together and issued separately in a single volume as *Complete Prefaces* (Constable, 1934; extended edition, Odhams Press, 1938). The other large, miscellaneous collection of essays and articles is *Doctors' Delusions, Crude Criminology, and Sham Education* (*Works*, Limited Edition, 1930, Standard Edition, 1931). Posthumous collections are: *The Religious Speeches of Bernard Shaw* (Pennsylvania University Press, 1963); *George Bernard Shaw on Language* (New York: Philosophical Library, 1963; London: Peter Owen, 1965); and *Shaw on Religion* (Constable, 1967).

The Adventures of the Black Girl in Her Search for God (Constable, 1932) really stands alone in Shaw's work as an extended humanist fable. He himself asociated it with a number of short fictions, such as 'Aerial Football', by including it in the collection, *Short Stories, Scraps and Shavings* (*Works*, Limited Edition, 1932, Standard Edition, 1934); it was reissued by Penguin Books, before his death, under a slightly changed title, in *The Black Girl in Search of God and Some Lesser Tales* (1946).

Shaw never wrote his autobiography, but produced a number of autobiographical fragments in his later years, collecting them as *Sixteen Self-Sketches* (*Works*, Standard Edition, 1949). Stanley Weintraub remedied Shaw's negligence by compiling scattered autobiographical comments from a wide assortment of his writings into *An Autobiography*, published in two volumes, covering 1856-1898 and 1898-1950 respectively (New York: Weybright and Talley, 1969 and 1970).

Letters

It has been estimated that Shaw wrote, on average, ten letters on each day of his adult life. A number of collections written to particular correspondents have already been published, and there are likely to be more in the future. The most celebrated is *Ellen Terry and Bernard Shaw: a Correspondence* (New York: Fountain Press; London: Constable, 1931) — the letters mostly having been written before the correspondents actually met. A substantial selection of unpublished and previously published letters is expertly and most helpfully edited by Dan H. Laurence in the authorized *Collected Letters*, in four volumes (London: Reinhardt, 1965, 1972, 1985, 1988).

The greatest story-tellers are the most inveterate moralists; and no man who is not an idiot can tell a story without shaping it in such a way as to move the sympathy of the audience by appealing to their moral ideas.

'Ten Minutes with Mr. Bernard Shaw',
To-Day, 28 Apr.1894

I am an advocate for stage illusion; stage realism is a contradiction in terms. I am only a realist in a Platonic sense.

As above

If you ask what my choice would be between 'four boards and a passion' and a sumptuous *mise-en-scène* without the passion, I am for the four boards. There is no rule that applies to all plays except the rule that no play should look shabby.

As above

My first three plays ... were what people call realistic. They were dramatic pictures of middle-class society from the point of view of a Socialist who regards the basis of that society as thoroughly rotten economically and morally. ... All three plays were criticisms of a special phase, the capitalist phase, of modern social organization, and their purpose was to make people thoroughly uncomfortable whilst entertaining them artistically.

Letter to R. Golding Bright, 10 June 1896,
Collected Letters, 1, p. 632

To me the tragedy and comedy of life lie in the consequences of our persistent attempts to found our institutions on the ideals suggested to our imaginations by our half-satisfied passions, instead of on a genuinely scientific natural history.

Preface to *Plays Pleasant and Unpleasant*,
Vol. II, 1898

My stories are the old stories; my characters are the familiar harlequin and columbine, clown and pantaloon, ... my stage tricks and surprises and thrills and jests are the ones in vogue when I was a boy, by which time my grandfather was tired of them.

Preface to *Three Plays for Puritans*, 1901

[*Shaw resorted to publishing his plays because of his difficulty in getting them performed. Here he comments on his habit of including lengthy directions.*] Let me give an example of a stage direction of my own which has been rebuked as a silly joke by people who do not understand the real relations of author and actor. It runs thus: '*So-and-so's complexion fades into stone-grey; and all movement and expression desert his eyes.*' This is the sort of stage direction an actor really wants. ... He can produce the impression suggested by the direction perfectly. *How* he produces it is his business, not mine. ...

It will often strain your ingenuity to describe a scene so that a stage manager can set it from the printed description, yet not a word is let slip that could remind the reader of the footlights. But it can be done: and the reward is that people can read your plays — even actor-managers. ...

'How to Make Plays Readable', *The Author*,
London, XII, Dec. 1901

I have given you a series of first-rate music hall entertainments, thinly disguised as plays, but really offering the public a unique string of turns by comics and serio-comics of every popular type. ... Make no error, ... that is the jam that has carried the propaganda pill down.

Letter to J. E. Vedrenne,
manager of the Court Theatre, Apr. 1907

[*The direction of most of Shaw's plays by the Vedrenne-Barker management at the Court Theatre, London, from 1904 to 1907, was usually a collaborative effort involving both the author and Granville Barker. This passage indicates their different contributions.*] I should have come up for the last few rehearsals: the combination works better than the single cylinder. ... A bit of training does them no harm, it will enable me to let them rip all the more recklessly next time.

Letter to Granville Barker, 19 Sept. 1907

[*On casting the plays.*] Leave me the drunken, stagey, brassbowelled barnstormers my plays are written for.

Letter to Granville Barker, 19 Jan. 1908

Surely nobody expects a play by me to have a plot. I am a dramatic poet, not a plot-monger.

Daily Telegraph, 7 May 1908,
reprinted in *Plays*, III (Bodley Head Shaw), p. 6

All the characters must be sympathetic. In fact, all the characters in all my plays must be sympathetic: what so often plays the devil with them on the stage is that the actors try to make butts of them, and imagine that what I am aiming at is personal ridicule and belittlement instead of the higher comedy in which the laugh is at the imperfections of our nature and the inadequacy of our institutions. ...

Letter to Augustin Hamon,
Shaw's French translator, 5 Nov. 1912

My plays bear very plain marks of my musical education. My deliberate rhetoric, and my reversion to the Shakespearian feature of long set roles for my characters, are pure Italian opera. My rejection of plot and *dénouement*, and my adoption of a free development of themes, are German symphony. My clown and ringmaster technique of discussion cannot be referred to French music: it is plain Molière; but I daresay I learned something from Gounod as well as from Fra Angelico as to the ease with which religious emotion and refined sexual emotion can be combined.

To Demetrius O'Bolger, his would-be biographer, Feb. 1916,
Collected Letters, 3, p. 374

[*The author and editor J. C. Squire had declared himself troubled by the change in Shaw's dramatic method.*] It will be all right when you realize that I am carrying on Soc[rates]' business, and not trying to be an almighty smart man of letters. ... My third manner is going to be more trying than my second; but then third manners always are. You are in your prime, and want second manner work — Eroica symphonies and such; but when you are 63 like me, you will have exhausted the second manner and care for nothing but third manner.

Letter to J. C. Squire, 14 Oct. 1919,
Collected Letters, 3, p. 636

Your chief artistic activity will be to prevent the actors taking their tone and speed from one another, instead of from their own parts, and thus destroying the continual variety and contrast which are the soul of liveliness in comedy and truth in tragedy.

Letter to Edward McNulty, 1922, published as
'On the Art of Rehearsal', *Arts League of Service Annual 1921-22*

My plays are not constructed plays: they grow naturally. ... Neither have I ever been what you call a representationist or realist. I was always in the classic tradition, recognizing that stage characters must be endowed by the author with a conscious self-knowledge and power of expression, and, as you observe with genuine penetration, a freedom from inhibitions, which in real life would make them monsters of genius.

Letter to Alexander Bashky, 24 May 1923,
printed in *The New York Times*, 12 June 1927

You are right in saying that my plays require a special technique of acting, and, in particular, great virtuosity in sudden transitions of mood that seem to the ordinary actor to be transitions from one 'line' of character to another. But, after all, this is only fully accomplished acting; for there is no other sort of acting except bad acting, acting that is the indulgence of imagination instead of the exercise of skill.

As above

I write plays that play for three hours and a half even with instantaneous changes and only one short interval. There is no time for silences or pauses: the actor must play on the line and not between the lines, and must do nine-tenths of his acting with his voice.

Letter to John Barrymore, 22 Feb. 1925,
Collected Letters, 3, p. 903

For the sake of the Maddermarket Theatre which Mr. Nugent Monck has made one of the most remarkable artistic theatres in England, I must not allow it to be supposed that the citizens of Norwich cannot enjoy themselves there, when one of my plays is being performed, unless they read a treatise of 30,000 words or so, first. ... I can assure them that most of the plays were written and performed long before the prefaces were thought of. ... I rather implore playgoers not to come to the play with their heads full of the preface, thereby confusing their attention by trying to discover relationships between the two that do not exist. The play is a work complete in itself; and so is the preface.

Letter to *Eastern Daily Press*, 17 Apr. 1928

Though my trade is that of a playwright, my vocation is that of a prophet, with occasional lapses into what ancient people call buffoonery.

Malvern Festival Book, 1932

In a generation which knew nothing of any sort of acting but drawing-room acting, and which considered a speech of more than twenty words impossibly long, I went back to the classical style and wrote long rhetorical speeches like operatic roles, regarding my plays as musical performances precisely as Shakespeare did. As a producer I went back to the forgotten heroic stage business and the exciting or impressive decla-

113

mation I had heard from old timers like Ristori, Salvini, and Barry Sullivan.

> Introduction to Lillah McCarthy, *Myself and My Friends*,
> London, Butterworth, 1933, p. 220-21

For broadcasting, the players, being invisible, must be specially careful not to imitate one another, nor to take their speed and pitch from one another, nor to race or rival one another, nor to pick up a cue and return it as a cricketer fields a ball as smartly and quickly as possible. ... An actor should always be surprised at what is said — delighted, disgusted, alarmed or what not as the case may be, but always a bit surprised, or taken aback enough to make the audience believe that it is unexpected.

> Letter to Edith Evans, 7 July 1942, quoted in
> Bryan Forbes, *Ned's Girl*, Elm Tree Books, 1977, p. 204

The perfect producer lets his actors act, and is their helper at need and not their dictator.

> 'Granville-Barker: Some Particulars',
> *Drama*, New Series, No. 3, Winter 1946

In selecting the cast no regard should be given to whether the actors understand the play or not. ... But their ages and personalities should be suitable, and their voices should not be alike. The four principals should be soprano, alto, tenor, and bass. Vocal contrast is of the greatest importance. ...

> 'Rules for Play Producers', *The Strand*, CXVII, July 1949

Opera taught me to shape my plays into recitatives, arias, duets, trios, ensemble finales and bravura pieces to display the technical accomplishments of the executants.

> *New Statesman and Nation*, 6 May 1950

Coda: Other Writers on Shaw's Work

A director cannot ignore many of [Shaw's] stage directions with impunity.

> Lee Simonson, *Parts of a Lifetime*,
> New York: Duell, Sloan, and Pearce, 1943, p. 51

You either lost interest in your last acts, or you were content with glaringly artificial devices. ... Then, when you found yourself independent of the ordinary manager and the ordinary public, you promptly threw plot overboard — no, I am wrong, you did it gradually — and at last convinced yourself that the ideal drama was a non-stop logomachy.

William Archer, to Shaw, 20 June 1923,
Collected Letters, 3, p. 836

To Shaw, careless speaking was as unpardonable as careless singing in opera.

Lewis Casson (actor in the Vedrenne-Barker Company),
'A Remembrance', in *Setting the Stage*,
Minneapolis: Tyrone Guthrie Theatre, 1966, p. 21

Given his cavalier confrontationalism as dramatist, his fervour as egalitarian moralist, it seems unpleasantly ironic that he should have been, for so long now, appropriated by the richest, glossiest, most commercial production companies for what is called 'revival'. The term suggests the dead, but Shaw's work didn't die. It just got gobbled up, assimilated in the treacly repertoire of plays considered suitable as 'star vehicles'.

Susan Todd, *New Statesman*, 25 May 1984

a: Primary Sources

Where no publisher is named below, the work was issued by Constable, London, Shaw's usual publisher during his lifetime. Place of publication is mentioned only when it was not London.

Before 1930, Shaw's plays appeared either in small collections, or singly, in order of composition: details are given in Section 2. These texts were reprinted, commonly in revised form, and others were added, in the main subsequent collections.

Principal Collected Editions

Limited Edition. *Collected Works*, in 30 volumes (1930-32), and three later volumes (1934, 1938, and 1938).

Standard Edition. *Collected Works*, in 37 volumes (1931-50).

Authorized Edition: *Collected Plays and Their Prefaces*, in seven volumes, under the editorial supervision of Dan H. Laurence (Max Reinhardt, 1970-74) — the 'Bodley Head Shaw'. [Previously unpublished texts are in Vol. VII, but ephemeral writings by Shaw relating to specific plays, are included in all volumes.]

Complete Plays, 1931; enlarged in successive reprints up to 1950, and also issued by Odhams Press for readers of *The Daily Herald*, 1934; new edition, Hamlyn, 1960, reprinted 1965. [This edition does not include Shaw's prefaces.]

Prefaces, 1934; enlarged, Odhams Press, 1938.

The Collected Screenplays, ed. Bernard F. Dukore. George Prior, 1980.

Early Texts: Play Manuscripts in Facsimile, in twelve volumes, with individual editors, under General Editorship of Dan H. Laurence. New York: Garland Publishing, 1981. [A facsimile edition for scholars.]

All the plays have additionally been published in paperback editions by Penguin Books, Harmondsworth, 1946-1985, and a substantial number, often in educational editions, also by Longman.

Posthumous Editions of Novels and Short Fiction

My Dear Dorothea: a Practical System of Moral Education for Females, with a Note by Stephen Winsten. Phoenix House, 1956. [Written in 1878.]

An Unfinished Novel, ed. Stanley Weintraub. Constable, 1958.

The Black Girl in Search of God, and Some Lesser Tales, corrected, definitive text, ed. Dan H. Laurence. Harmondsworth: Penguin, 1977.

Cashel Byron's Profession, new edition, supervised by Dan H. Laurence. Harmondsworth: Penguin, 1979.

An Unsocial Socialist, with Introduction by Michael Holroyd. Virago Modern Classics, 1980.

Posthumous Editions of Essays, Speeches, Criticism

Plays and Players: Essays on the Theatre, selected by A. C. Ward. Oxford University Press, 1952 (World's Classics).

Shaw on the Theatre, ed. E. J. West. New York: Hill and Wang, 1958; London: McGibbon and Kee, 1960. [Most items not previously collected.]

How to Become a Musical Critic, ed. Dan H. Laurence. Hart-Davis, 1961. [Anthology of Shaw's music criticism, 1876-1950.]

Shaw on Shakespeare, ed. Edwin Wilson. New York: Dutton, 1961; London: Cassell, 1962.

Platform and Pulpit, ed. Dan H. Laurence. Hart-Davis, 1962. [Previously uncollected lectures and speeches.]

The Matter with Ireland, ed. Dan H. Laurence and David H. Greene. New York: Hill and Wang; Hart-Davis, 1962. [Mainly uncollected writings and speeches relating to Ireland.]

The Religious Speeches of Bernard Shaw, ed. Warren Sylvester Smith. University Park, Pennsylvania: Pennsylvania State University Press, 1963.

On Language, ed. Abraham Tauber, with a foreword by Sir James Pitman. New York: Philosophical Library, 1963; London: Peter Owen, 1965.

Shaw on Religion, ed. Warren Sylvester Smith. Constable, 1967. [A distinct collection from *The Religious Speeches.*]

The Road to Equality, ten unpublished lectures and essays, 1884-1918, ed. Louis Crompton. Boston: Beacon Press, 1971.

Bernard Shaw's Non-Dramatic Literary Criticism, ed. Stanley Weintraub. Lincoln: University of Nebraska Press, 1972.

Bernard Shaw's Practical Politics: Views on Politics and Economics, ed. Lloyd J. Hubenka. Lincoln: University of Nebraska Press, 1976. [All items collected here for the first time.]

The Portable Bernard Shaw, ed. Stanley Weintraub. New York: Viking Press; Harmondsworth: Penguin, 1977.

The Great Composers: Reviews and Bombardments, ed. Louis Crompton. Berkeley; London: University of California Press, 1978.

Shaw and Ibsen, ed. J. L. Wisenthal. Toronto; Buffalo; London: University of Toronto Press, 1979. [A new edition of *The Quintessence of Ibsenism*, with shorter items collected for the first time.]

Shaw's Music, in three volumes, ed. Dan H. Laurence. 'The Bodley Head Shaw', Max Reinhardt, 1981. [Collected musical criticism.]

Major Critical Essays, with an introduction by Michael Holroyd. Harmondsworth: Penguin, 1986. [New edition of work first published in 1891, containing *The Quintessence of Ibsenism, The New Perfect Wagnerite*, and *The Sanity of Art*.]

Shaw on Dickens, ed. Dan H. Laurence and Martin Quinn. New York: Ungar, 1984.

Autobiography

Shaw: an Autobiography, 1856-1898. Selected from his writings by Stanley Weintraub. New York: Weybright and Talley, 1969; London: Max Reinhardt, 1970.

Shaw: an Autobiography, 1898-1950 — the Playwright Years. Selected from his writings by Stanley Weintraub. New York: Weybright and Talley, 1970; London: Max Reinhardt, 1971.

Letters

Collected Letters, authorized edition by Dan H. Laurence, Vol. I, 1874-1897; Vol. II, 1898-1910; Vol. III, 1911-1925; Vol. IV, 1926-1950. Max Reinhardt, 1965, 1972, 1985, 1988. [A generous selection, excellently annotated, including some (but not all) letters from the separate collections listed below, which are much concerned with theatrical matters.]

Letters ... to Miss Alma Murray. Edinburgh: privately printed, 1927.

Ellen Terry and Bernard Shaw: a Correspondence. New York: Fountain Press; London: Constable, 1931; second edition, Reinhardt 1949.

More Letters ... to Miss Alma Murray. Edinburgh: privately printed, 1952.

Florence Farr, Bernard Shaw, W.B. Yeats: Letters, ed. Clifford Bax. Dublin: Cuala Press, 1941; London, 1946; Shannon: Irish University Press, 1971.

Bernard Shaw and Mrs. Patrick Campbell: Their Correspondence,
   ed. Alan Dent. Gollancz, 1952.

Advice to a Young Critic: Letters to Golding Bright, ed. E. J. West. New
   York: Crown Publishers, 1955; London: Peter Owen, 1956.

Letters to Granville Barker, ed. C. B. Purdom. Rockliff, 1957. [What
   survives of the other half of this correspondence is included in
   Chapter III of *Granville Barker and His Correspondents*, ed. Eric
   Salmon (Detroit: Wayne State University Press, 1986), p. 116-63.]

Letters to Edith Evans, in Bryan Forbes, *Ned's Girl*. (Elm Tree Books,
   1977).

Shaw's Letters to Siegfried Trebitsch, ed. Samuel A. Weiss. Stanford,
   California: Stanford University Press, 1986. [Trebitsch was
   authorized translator of Shaw's plays into German.]

The Playwright and the Pirate. Bernard Shaw and Frank Harris: a
   Correspondence, ed. Stanley Weintraub. Gerrards Cross: Colin
   Smythe, 1982. [This and the following two items are of less
   specifically theatrical interest.]

Bernard Shaw and Alfred Douglas: a Correspondence, ed. Mary Hyde.
   John Murray, 1982.

Agitations: Letters to the Press, 1875-1950, ed. Dan H. Laurence.
   New York: Ungar, 1985.

Diaries

Bernard Shaw's Diaries, ed. Stanley Weintraub. University Park,
   Pennsylvania: Pennsylvania State University Press, 1985.

Adaptations

My Fair Lady. A musical play in two acts based on Shaw's *Pygmalion*.
   Adaptation and lyrics by Alan J. Lerner. Harmondsworth: Penguin,
   1956. [Authorization of this was accompanied by an embargo on
   productions of *Pygmalion*, now lifted. There have been a number of
   other adaptations of Shaw's works — plays into musicals, letters into
   plays, etc. — not all of them authorized.]

b: Secondary Sources

Biography

Archibald Henderson, *G. B. Shaw: His Life and Works*. Hurst and
Blackett, 1911. [Directly dependent on information from Shaw, as
were the same author's *Bernard Shaw: Playboy and Prophet*
(New York; London: Appleton, 1932), and *George Bernard Shaw:
Man of the Century* (New York: Appleton-Century-Crofts, 1956).]

Frank Harris, *Bernard Shaw: an Unauthorized Biography*, with a
Postscript by Shaw. Gollancz, 1931.

St. John Ervine, *Bernard Shaw, His Life, Work and Friends*.
Constable, 1956.

B. C. Rossett, *Shaw of Dublin: the Formative Years*. University Park:
Pennsylvania State University Press, 1964.

John O'Donovan, *Shaw*. Dublin; London: Gill and Macmillan, 1983
(Irish Lives series).

Margot Peters, *Bernard Shaw and the Actresses*. Garden City,
New York: Doubleday, 1980. [Also a critical study.]

Michael Holroyd, *Shaw*, Vol. I. Chatto and Windus, 1988. [This
authorized biography, now in progress, will, when complete,
supersede all the earlier attempts noted above.]

A. M. Gibbs, ed., *Bernard Shaw: Interviews and Recollections*.
Macmillan, forthcoming.

Stage History

Desmond MacCarthy, *The Court Theatre, 1904-07: a Commentary and
a Criticism*. A. H. Bullen, 1907; reissued, with a commentary by
Stanley Weintraub, Coral Gables: Florida: Miami University Press,
1966.

G. W. Bishop, *Barry Jackson and the London Theatre*. Arthur Barker,
1933.

T. C. Kemp, *Birmingham Repertory Theatre*. Birmingham: Cornish
Brothers, 1943.

Richard Huggett, *The Truth about Pygmalion*. Heinemann, 1969. [On
the 1914 London production.]

Erwin Stürzl and James Hogg, *The Stage History of Bernard Shaw's
Saint Joan*. Salzburg: Institüt für Englische Sprache und Literatur,
1975.

J. L. Styan, *Modern Drama in Theory and Practice*, Vols. I and II.
Cambridge University Press, 1981.

Bernard F. Dukore, comp., *Arms and the Man: a Composite Production Book*. Carbondale, Illinois: Southern Illinois Press, 1982.

See also: Mander and Mitchenson, *A Theatrical Companion to Shaw*, under 'Reference Sources', p. 123 below.

Selected Critical Studies

J. G. Huneker, *Iconoclasts*. T. Werner Laurie, 1906. [Chapter on Shaw.]

G. K. Chesterton, *George Bernard Shaw*. John Lane, 1909; new edition, with additional chapter, 1935; various later reprints.

P. P. Howe, *Bernard Shaw: a Critical Study*. Martin Secker, 1915.

Martin Ellehauge, *The Position of Bernard Shaw in European Drama and Philosophy*. Copenhagen: Levin and Munksgaard, 1931.

E. Strauss, *Bernard Shaw: Art and Socialism*. Gollancz, 1942; new edition, 1978.

Eric Bentley, *Bernard Shaw*. Norfolk, Connecticut: New Directions Books, 1947; London: Robert Hale, 1950; revised edition, 1957; reissued 1967, 1976 (Norton Press).

Francis Fergusson, *The Idea of a Theater*. Princeton, N.J.: Princeton University Press, 1949; reprinted frequently. [Includes a stimulating, if sometimes perverse, discussion of *Major Barbara* and *Heartbreak House* as variants of drawing-room comedy.]

William Irvine, *The Universe of GBS*. New York: McGraw-Hill, 1949.

Alick West, *A Good Man Fallen among Fabians*. Lawrence and Wishart, 1950; new edition, 1974. [Unusually perceptive marxist criticism, especially interesting on the novels and plays up to *Major Barbara*.]

Desmond MacCarthy, *Shaw*. Macgibbon and Kee, 1951; American edition entitled *Shaw's Plays in Review*. [Collected reviews, mainly of the first productions.]

J. B. Kaye, *Bernard Shaw and the Nineteenth-Century Tradition*. Norman, Oklahoma: University of Oklahoma Press, 1958.

Martin Meisel, *Shaw and the Nineteenth-Century Theater*. Princeton University Press; Oxford University Press, 1963. [Begins new movement in scholarly criticism concentrating on the plays through their theatrical context.]

Robert Brustein, *The Theatre of Revolt*. Boston: Little, Brown, 1964; London: Methuen, 1965. [Chapter on Shaw: popularized the charge that, by refusing to face the truth of his own feelings, Shaw lost the possibility of tragic vision.]

Barbara Bellew Watson, *A Shavian Guide to the Intelligent Woman*. Chatto and Windus, 1964.

Harold Fromm, *Bernard Shaw and the Theater in the Nineties: a Study of Shaw's Dramatic Criticism*. Lawrence, Kansas, 1967.

Charles A. Carpenter, *Bernard Shaw and the Art of Destroying Ideals*. Madison, Wisconsin: University of Wisconsin Press, 1969. [The early plays.]

Louis Crompton, *Shaw the Dramatist*. Lincoln, Nebraska: University of Nebraska Press, 1969.

A. M. Gibbs, *Shaw*. Edinburgh: Oliver and Boyd, 1969. [A short but pithy critical study.]

Colin Wilson, *Bernard Shaw: a Reassessment*. Hutchinson, 1969. [General study.]

Elsie B. Adams, *Bernard Shaw and the Aesthetes*. Columbus, Ohio: Ohio State University Press, 1971.

Margery M. Morgan, *The Shavian Playground: an Exploration of the Art of G. B. Shaw*. Methuen, 1972.

Charles A. Berst, *Bernard Shaw and the Art of Drama*. Urbana, Illinois: University of Missouri Press, 1973.

Maurice J. Valency, *The Cart and the Trumpet: the Plays of Bernard Shaw*. New York: Oxford University Press, 1973.

J. L. Wisenthal, *The Marriage of Contraries: Bernard Shaw's Middle Plays*. Cambridge, Mass.: Harvard University Press, 1974.

Alfred Turco, *Shaw's Moral Vision*. Ithaca, New York: Cornell University Press, 1976.

R. F. Whitman, *Shaw and the Play of Ideas*. Ithaca, New York: Cornell University Press, 1977.

Margery M. Morgan, *Bernard Shaw*, in two volumes: Vol. I, 1856-1907; Vol. II, 1907-1950. Windsor, Berks.: Profile Books, 1982 (Writers and Their Work series). [General introduction, with bibliography.]

Arthur Ganz, *George Bernard Shaw*. Macmillan, 1983 (Modern Dramatists series).

A. M. Gibbs, *The Art and Mind of Shaw: Essays in Criticism*. Macmillan, 1983.

Nicholas Greene, *Bernard Shaw: a Critical View*. Macmillan, 1984 (Studies in Anglo-Irish Literature series).

Keith M. May, *Ibsen and Shaw*. Macmillan, 1985.

Collections of Critical Essays

GBS 90: Aspects of Bernard Shaw's Life and Works, ed. Stephen Winsten. Hutchinson, 1936; reprinted, New York: Haskell House. [Contributors include Gilbert Murray, John Masefield, Sidney Webb, H. G. Wells, Max Beerbohm, Maynard Keynes, and others.]

George Bernard Shaw: a Critical Survey, ed. L. Kronenberger.
New York; Cleveland: World Publishing, 1953. [Contributions by
W. H. Auden, Eric Bentley, Max Beerbohm, G. K. Chesterton,
V. S. Pritchett, and others.]

Twentieth-Century Views of George Bernard Shaw, ed. R. J. Kaufmann.
Englewood Cliffs, New Jersey: Prentice-Hall, 1965.

Shaw: Seven Critical Essays, ed. Norman Rosenblood. Toronto;
Buffalo: Toronto University Press, 1971. [Includes a long essay,
'Shaw and Revolution: the Politics of the Plays', by M. Meisel. Other
contributors are Alan Downer, Stanley Weintraub, R. B. Parker,
Warren S. Smith, J. D. Merritt, and Clifford Leech.]

T. F. Evans, ed., *Shaw: the Critical Heritage*. Routledge and Kegan
Paul, 1976. [Selections from early reviews of each play, both on the
stage and on the page.]

The Genius of Bernard Shaw, ed. Michael Holroyd. Hodder and
Stoughton, 1979. [The contributors are J. O'Donovan, T. de Vere
White, S. Weintraub, C. Osborne, J. S. Collis, Brigid Brophy,
R. Skidelsky, H. Spurling, I. Wardle, M. Peters, Benny Green,
Barbara Smoker, and M. Holroyd.]

Fabian Feminist, ed. Rodelle Weintraub. University Park: Pennsylvania
State University Press, 1976. [Contributors include Lisë Pedersen,
Norbert Greiner, B. B. Watson, Elsie Adams, and Germaine Greer.
There is also material by Shaw himself.]

*Studies in Edwardian and Anglo-Irish Drama: Cahiers Victoriens et
Edwardiens*, Nos. 9-10, ed. J. C. Amalric. Montpellier, France,
Oct. 1979. [Contributors on Shaw are H. F. Salerno, Rodelle
Weintraub, Margery Morgan, J. C. Amalric, Pierre Vitoux, and
F. P. W. McDowell.]

The Annual of Bernard Shaw Studies, 3: Shaw's Plays in Performance,
ed. Daniel Leary. University Park; London: Pennsylvania State
University Press, 1983. [Contributors include Leary, Berst, Whitman,
T. F. Evans, R. Hornby, Dukore, etc., and there are also reported
interviews with Lillah McCarthy and Ann Casson. There is relevant
material in the other volumes of this series.]

Reference Sources

Raymond Mander and Joe Mitchenson, *A Theatrical Companion to
Shaw*. Rockliff, 1954; reissued in larger format, Norwood Editions,
1977. [Indispensable, and a primary source for the present book.
Sadly, the many illustrations are poorly reproduced in the reissue.]

E. Dean Bevan, *A Concordance to the Plays and Prefaces of Bernard*

Shaw, in ten volumes. Detroit: Gale, 1971. [References are to the Standard Edition of the works.]

Dan H. Laurence, *Bernard Shaw: a Bibliography*, in two volumes. Oxford University Press, 1983 (The Soho Bibliographies). [The definitive, scholarly work of reference on all Shaw's writings.]

Shaw: an Annotated Bibliography of Writings about Him, in three volumes: Vol. I, ed. J. P. Wearing; Vol. III, ed. D. Haberman. Northern Illinois University Press, 1986 and 1985 respectively. [Vol III not seen; Vol II not yet available.]